A Guide to Designing Research Questions for Beginning Music Therapy Researchers

Katrina S. McFerran, PhD, RMT
University of Melbourne, Australia

Michael J. Silverman, PhD, MT-BC
University of Minnesota, USA

The American Music Therapy Association is a non-profit association dedicated to increasing access to quality music therapy services for individuals with disabilities or illnesses or for those who are interested in personal growth and wellness. AMTA provides extensive educational and research information about the music therapy profession. Referrals for qualified music therapists are also provided to consumers and parents. AMTA holds an annual conference every autumn and its eight regions hold conferences every spring. For up-to-date information, please access the AMTA website at www.musictherapy.org

ISBN: 978-1-884914-36-2

The American Music Therapy Association, Inc.
8455 Colesville Rd., Suite 1000
Silver Spring, MD 20910

Phone: (301) 589-3300
Fax: (301) 589-5175
Email: info@musictherapy.org
Website: www.musictherapy.org

Cover design — GrassT Design
Technical assistance and formatting — Wordsetters, Inc.
Layout design — GrassT Design

Printed in the United States of America

A Guide to Designing Research Questions for Beginning Music Therapy Researchers

Katrina S. McFerran, PhD, RMT
University of Melbourne, Australia

Michael J. Silverman, PhD, MT-BC
University of Minnesota, USA

AMERICAN
MUSIC
THERAPY
ASSOCIATION ®

Contents

Preface

We begin this book with a personal narrative that contextualizes our writing of the chapters and our respect for a range of research traditions. The full text of this preface may be of interest to some readers. Others may glance through the paragraph headings. It may be of no interest to other readers, in which case, they may continue on to Chapter 1, where the body of the text begins.

We met at an international research conference in Korea.

This point is critical to our rationale for writing this introductory textbook. We were both attending the conference because we are interested in what our international colleagues are doing in both research and clinical practice. We want to contribute to the largest international discussion of research that is available and to bring what we learn back to our own places to share. To that end, we take opportunities to travel long distances, to stay in impersonal hotel rooms, and to reach out to our colleagues at breaks and over meals because we want to learn more about music therapy research.

Before ever speaking to one another, we knew that our research approaches were very different.

Meeting and talking with research colleagues about research is one thing, but this cannot happen in a meaningful way unless we have read the works of those people and therefore have a basis for our conversation. Both of us enjoy writing, so there was plenty of literature for us to read that had been written by the other, and we had an overlapping interest in mental health. Mike had already contributed to the literature a range of investigations about the effectiveness of music therapy in adult acute mental health settings, and Kat had published studies using qualitative data that emphasized the meaning made by participants about music therapy.

We independently attended one another's presentations, to see what the other had to say.

There are limits to how much you can know about a researcher's stance from the way they[1] write their articles. Although belief systems are reflected in the choices we make about designs and the style of our writing, these features also reflect the requirements of

---

[1] Throughout the text, we purposely use nonbinary personal pronouns in order to include a range of gender identities. We have been inspired in particular by "radical" copyeditor, Alex Kapitan, whose guidance on bias-free and respectful language in reference to transgender people is clear, cogent, and caring. Kapitan suggests we "respect singular *they* as a personal pronoun and use it accordingly" (https://radicalcopyeditor.com/2017/08/31/transgender-style-guide/). We have taken this advice.

journals and academic discourse. We both wanted to know if the other person was open to a range of ways of understanding music therapy, or was interested in only one way—their own. The fact that we were both at the conference, in a country other than our own, made us optimistic that this discourse might be possible.

Mike clearly believed in his approach but did not overestimate its significance.

When I listened to Mike's talk, I could hear that he was excited to present the results of his research, but he knew its limitations. Moreover, he was aware of how his studies were situated in the contextual parameters that were idiosyncratic to acute mental health care in the United States. He clearly realized that he could not generalize based on a limited sample size. He also referred to the work of other researchers and was equally positive about their contributions. This included a range of studies by people from different backgrounds and research approaches.

Kat was passionate about her work with adolescents but understood its context in the literature base.

Although I was familiar with Kat's published work and admired it, I purposely sought out her presentations at conferences to hear her speak. Her work contained such wonderful depth and appropriately drew from related disciplines. I enjoyed listening to her engaging narratives and quickly understood why she was such a great researcher and mentor for her students. After hearing her speak, I was remotivated to contribute to the literature to help those receiving music therapy. Highlighting users' stories, Kat undoubtedly believed in her work and the significance of it, and clearly articulated what it was—and was not—capable of achieving within the larger literature base.

Our goals to provide increased access to music therapy services were similar, but we were cognizant that it takes a village, not a vacuum.

We both recognized that a single music therapy study will not change music therapy practice, how funding is allocated, or how to conduct future studies. Research does not exist in a vacuum—it builds upon itself with both breadth and depth. Thus, regardless of approach, data type, or mode of inquiry, we appreciated each other's work and were keenly aware of where it stood and what it meant for our literature.

Over the next few years we met briefly at conferences around the world.

One of the advantages of working at research-focused universities is that we are encouraged to engage with international colleagues. With the support of our universities and families, we have both been able to attend many international conferences in order to contribute to academic discourse and to learn about studies before they are published. We both have young families, so it is not always easy to be away from home, but it is a priority and a privilege to have the opportunity to visit different countries and participate in the diverse music therapy cultures that exist.

During one exchange about different research methodologies, we began to discuss teaching students to write their first research question.

Both of us are responsible for teaching introduction to music therapy research classes in master's coursework programs. We were excited about the latest edition of the classic *Music Therapy Research* text, edited by Barbara Wheeler and Kathleen Murphy[2] (2016), but we felt there was still a gap in the literature about how to identify and successively narrow the topic of a first music therapy research project. We discussed the challenges of teaching students to appreciate the importance of the research question, and we began to share strategies that we had used previously.

*We talked about the idea that **the research question always drives the method**.*

This is a commonly accepted statement, and it was endorsed in the most recent music therapy research textbook, where Alice-Ann Darrow (2016) noted, "Stating the research problem as a question indicates the type of data that will be collected and the method of analysis" (p. 51). However, Kat argued that beginning researchers do not craft an elegant and articulate question, such as "What is the experience of group music therapy for six younger bereaved adolescents?" without intending to use, or being guided toward using, phenomenological approaches. Mike agreed that his students also needed help to construct questions, such as "Are there between-group coping self-efficacy differences in adult acute care mental health patients who receive music therapy and those in a control group?" This kind of question is already informed by a range of beliefs that have been popularized in an evidence-based culture, the details of which may not have much meaning yet for the student.

We felt the purpose of writing a great research question was more than choosing the right method.

Kat had previously encouraged a graduate researcher to write about her experience of transitioning from clinical experiences to clinical questions and the development of a research question (Roberts, 2006). From this experience, Kat had developed an idea that many people were largely unconscious of their motivations for conducting research on various topics and how they did this, and she had explored this notion in subsequent supervision practices by encouraging new researchers to explore this more thoroughly.

---

[2] We deliberately chose to include authors' first names to make the authors more identifiable by markers such gender and culture, otherwise there is a tendency to assume that an author is a white man. Readers should be aware that in APA Style (http://www.apastyle.org), authors' first names or initials are typically not used in the prose or citations.

We turned to the literature to see who else had explored this conundrum.

While discussing the complexities of developing and narrowing research questions with a graduate student, Mike found an article by social scientist Kristin Luker (2008), who suggested to "ignore the taken-for-granted assumption that it (*the research question*) comes first" (p. 61) and instead focus on exploring the "intellectual itch" (p. 62) in order to transform that into a research question. Additionally, Mike frequently quoted Robert Duke (2010), who believed the construction of research questions is informed by a range of motivations. Duke described it this way:

> Discussions of research in our discipline often begin like this, with focus on the methods of research rather than on the problems the researcher is seeking to solve. This creates mistaken views of what the task is about. When the goal of research is to explain something, then the methods used to develop an explanation are selected to accomplish the goal of understanding. The questions suggest the methodology, but it's the questions that matter most. (p. 213)

This led us to a new point of inquiry: What factors do we perceive as influencing the development of the research question?

For us, as researchers, many interesting experiences have potential to become research projects, and in our minds, that was the next logical step. We were unable to find anything that satisfied our own intellectual itch, so we decided to proceed with an intersubjective examination of our own beliefs and experiences of mentoring students to develop research questions. We hoped to generate a clear framework to support students in this journey and planned to summarize the results of our inquiry in a journal article. However, our attempts to do that were unsatisfactory and, ultimately, we felt the "method" of our investigation was less important than the desire to explain our results in detail. So, the idea of a book for new researchers was born.

Our first step was to generate a long list of factors that we each thought influenced the development of a research question.

We began to discuss the research question as a communicative tool for sharing ideas with the scholarly community. This highlighted how each research question is actually embedded in a long tradition of a particular type of research, and those familiar with that type of research would immediately recognize key words and phrases. For example, a simple word like *effectiveness* cannot be included in a research question that does not quantitatively measure the outcome in some way. Similarly, asking about a person's *experience* of music therapy suggests that it cannot be reduced to numbers to be averaged or compared, as it needs to contain rich descriptions to understand the meaning associated with the experience. We realized that we knew these things because we were a part of the traditions of research, but students did not, since these words are also used in everyday language with considerably different meanings associated. Although at that point we did not know how the process would proceed, we had begun to develop, uncover, and study some of the hidden factors that influence the creation of research questions.

The next step included identifying a range of what we initially termed internal and external factors.

This included influences such as our academic training and preferences for different journals and publishers, our experiences of music therapy practice, including our theoretical preferences for cognitive behavioral, psychodynamic, humanistic, and ecological approaches, as well as our personalities and family backgrounds. We were also conscious of the external influences such as the expectations of our universities for publishing in high-impact journals, the belief systems that were dominant in the kinds of institutions we worked in, our access to potential research participants and collaborators, and the ethical considerations implicated in each of these contexts. We continued to write and rewrite lists of factors and descriptions of what we meant until we reached saturation and were unable to identify any more.

We decided that the internal factors were the most interesting to explore further and began to categorize them.

At this point, we conceived the factors as being related to either the participants in our research projects, our own values, and our beliefs about knowledge. Within each of these groups, we identified subcategories that further detailed what the factors actually were and how they interfaced with the creation of the research question and the decisions about methodology. However, we soon discovered that the discussion was incomplete without the inclusion of the external factors, as internal and external factors inevitably interacted with each other. This realization led us to think about each category as a layer in order to visually depict the overlap.

Each of the categories we generated appeared to be nested, with all connecting at a tangent that intersects with the creation of the research question and associated methodology.

The mathematical term for circles that intersect at a mutual tangent is *kissing circles*, which highlights how each layer has points of agreement and dynamic boundaries, rather than being rigid or detached layers. The boundaries between layers are porous, but we liked how this model distinguished the different layers and therefore made them more visible. We were also influenced by Urie Bronfenbrenner's ecological systems theory that describes how characteristics of the external environment interact with the internal qualities of a child and places the closest relationships at the center and the most distance at the outer layers. The result was a model (see Figure 1 in Chapter 1) that helped us to separate and discuss a number of hidden factors without suggesting that they were necessarily discrete.

The research question and associated method do not come one before the other; they have a symbiotic relationship.

Rather than the research question dictating the method, or the method shaping the research question, we perceive the influence of a range of intersecting factors that all shape the creation of the research question, which inherently contains pointers to the method. Although this might be implied in many research texts, we had not read a description of this as a symbiotic relationship; instead, we had always heard it referred to as occurring in a sequence.

We recognized that many aspects of our thinking were influenced by the philosophy of science.

Both of us had drawn on ideas from the philosophy of science in our teaching and had discovered ways of making these ideas accessible to new researchers. We felt that many Australian and American students had less pre-existing knowledge about philosophical ideas than some students from other parts of the world, and we wanted to incorporate these ideas into our explanation, using language that would be more familiar. Since we had both been Australian or American students once, we knew that it was more complex to grasp some ideas about the philosophy of science without a broad base of understanding of philosophy generally. We were uneasy about our own ability to convey these ideas in a way that engaged beginning research students without this background but have made our best attempt.

As music therapy academics at research-intensive universities, we both enjoy roles as researchers, clinicians, and educators.

This had been our initial point of connection and suggested that the outcome of our inquiry would be in a form that combined these interests and was helpful to our research students. After over two years of discussions via Skype, email, and occasional conference meet-ups, as well as an initial attempt to explain our ideas in a journal article, we agreed that an introductory textbook published by the American Music Therapy Association would be the most satisfying venue to express our ideas.

The primary purpose of the text is to help beginning researchers navigate through their research interests and arrive at a research question and associated method.

In the following chapters, we will elaborate the various hidden factors in ways that we hope will help students arrive at a practical, realistic, and intriguing research question. By offering illustrative examples, exercises, and explanations to engage you in different ways, we want to help you holistically understand the process and product associated with the task of developing a research question.[3] We hope that you will better understand

---

[3] We want to make the writing style of the book informal and conversational, as this is how research questions develop. We find that open conversation can facilitate the process of being amicable to new ways of thinking.

your own interests, motivations, beliefs, and values as a result of reading. We believe this will lead to better research experiences for you and contributions for the profession to ultimately increase access to care for users of music therapy services and to provide a more thorough understanding of the complex field that is music therapy.

Our own experiences of research have been engaging and intriguing, as has writing this book.

Although the research process that informed the material for this book was familiar to Kat, the intensely iterative and intersubjective process was more extreme than any form of interpretivist research Mike had previously experienced. It has been an epic journey for two people from two different countries and genders, with vastly different research backgrounds. Our commitment to the project has helped us to better understand one another's perspectives, as well as learn how to more clearly articulate our own. Every pre-assumption that each of us held about what was fundamental to shaping a research question has been challenged, deepened, and, occasionally, revised. We both continue to enjoy our own positions and are pleased to have grown in our understanding of our colleagues and our future research students.

Chapter 1
A Realistic Introduction to Research and the Importance of Research Questions

Introduction to the Text

The terminal product of this guidebook is intended to be an intriguing and feasible research question and associated method. As this is a successive process, each chapter is designed to narrow and refine your ideas as you consider a number of factors that can influence your project. Recognizing and working with these factors will sustain the development of your project as unanticipated issues, questions, and complications occur. This guidebook should set you up for success by helping you navigate the complexities of your initial journey into research before anything becomes problematic.

You may think that whenever a researcher conducts a project, it turns immediately to gold, such as a published research article that instantly garners the attention and admiration of the profession. However, what is not so obvious are the countless hours dedicated to designing projects, anticipating potential problems, running into problems, and modifying the project due to the problems encountered. Experienced researchers are continually learning about the processes and products associated with research, and a part of the excitement resulting from the research is knowing that this learning will never end. Although the journal article that reports on the project appears neat and clean to readers, there was likely a plethora of manuscript versions that were critiqued by peers and reviewers in order to arrive at the published product. So, as you embark on your first research project, we suggest it is helpful to remain humble and patient, because your process will probably be complex and exciting, with ups and downs along the journey.

It is also important to have realistic expectations throughout the various stages of your first research project. This is especially true during the initial conceptualization stages (notice how "stages" is plural). Your project is not intended to be "the study to end all studies" or the study to show that "Yes, music therapy works!" Rather, your first research experience will be just that—a first research experience. It is helpful to remain realistic and not put undue pressure on yourself. Quality typically comes with quantity, and your advisor—who remains the best person to ask any question related to your project—will ensure that the project has enough quality to earn a passing grade.

A Positive Research Mindset

How you conceptualize research, and all the various processes and products that comprise research, can have a lasting impact on your perceptions of the educational experience that you have during your first research project. Research is best approached with a positive, curious, and realistic mindset. It can be an enjoyable process, but—as with anything else—you have to consciously choose a stance that will facilitate this. Alternately, research can be a lot of hard work with very little pleasure, especially if you set expectations that are unlikely to be achieved. Gerry Mullins and Margaret Kiley[1] (2002) describe this concept for researchers at the PhD level, noting,

> A PhD is a stepping stone into a research career. All you need to do is to demonstrate your capacity of independent, critical thinking. That's all you need to do. A PhD is three years of solid work, not a Nobel Prize. (p. 386)

If you are conducting a research project as part of an undergraduate or master's level program, then these words are wiser still.

Similar to choosing happiness throughout the process of research, we can choose to be positive and supportive to our research peers. Being open to new ideas and supportive to your peers can benefit you as the researcher by making the process enjoyable for all involved. A number of years ago, Clifford Madsen (1974) articulated the importance of keeping our minds open throughout research processes and our careers:

> The intention is that, as we strive for greater scientific truth, we do not give credence only to our own closed system and so confound our methodology and confuse our purposes that we make a closed religious system out of our own particular brand of science. Indeed, it is hoped that we never perpetuate our own research to the exclusion of thought or in any other way reinforce our own behavior to the point where we truly believe that "no one knows research but me." (p. 180)

We have been fortunate to mentor many students through the research process—from initial conception of the project to a published manuscript and/or thesis. Throughout this process, we continually observe a few traits and factors that result in a more enjoyable process and product: tenacity, creativity, and thoughtfulness.

---

[1] We deliberately chose to include authors' first names to make the authors more identifiable by markers such as gender and culture, otherwise there may be a tendency to make incorrect assumptions. Readers should be aware that in APA Style (http://www.apastyle.org), authors' first names or initials are typically not used in the prose or citations.

Tenacity: We suggest that tenacity is the most crucial trait of a researcher. Research is not, and should not be, easy. A determined yet patient attitude will help you, as the researcher, to continue on your journey despite adversity, barriers, and unanticipated problems. This guidebook is designed to help you anticipate challenges that might occur and work in a preventative manner, rather than having to intervene after a major problem has occurred. How you respond to various problems is a critical factor for maintaining a positive research attitude and enjoying the process. Without the determined perseverance of researchers, difficult questions would likely remain unanswered.

Creativity: Research represents both a creative process and a creative product. Studying if, how, and why music therapy might be valuable for service users requires that we be continually open to new ways of thinking. Specific designs can be effective for answering specific research questions, and directing your creativity toward your curiosities can lead to interesting new discoveries. For example, it is important to recognize that not everything can—or should—be studied or understood with a randomized controlled trial. For instance, working alliance is widely recognized as the most predictive indicator of change in psychotherapeutic studies. However, by definition, one cannot study working alliance by comparing a group that receives music therapy with a control group (who receives nothing) because there is no working alliance in the control group—working alliance simply cannot be compared to a no-contact control group using that type of design. Therefore, a potential creative solution to studying working alliance in music therapy would be to have expert music therapists watch staged videos with varying levels of musicianship and verbal therapeutic interactions within the music therapy. Observers would then quantitatively or qualitatively rate the alliance between clients and the music therapist and then participate in a focus group to discuss elements of the music therapy that positively contributed to the working alliance. Thus, creative adoptions and adaptations to research questions and methods might need to be instituted in order to study elusive and challenging psychotherapeutic factors, such as working alliance.

Thoughtfulness: Quality research projects will challenge you to alter and expand your ways of thinking and how you conceptualize using music for health and well-being. It can be helpful to adopt an attitude of mindful consideration throughout the various stages of the research journey. As others will undoubtedly be involved in your project, it is imperative to remain kind and respectful to service users, staff, clinicians, administrators, Institutional Review/Ethics Board members, peer reviewers, and your advisor throughout adversities during your research. Respecting others' time and contributions can establish and maintain supportive conditions. Additionally, aspects of your project might seem overwhelming, so being patient and remaining open to new ideas as they emerge will help realize alternatives, results, and implications.

Defining Research

Research is a word that has numerous definitions and usages, largely dependent upon contexts. In fact, it can be used as both a verb and noun. For example, when a person states that they[2] are "researching the best car to purchase," the term *research* is not consistent with the expectations of a randomized controlled trial or interpretative phenomenological analysis. Instead, research likely means comparing vehicles online (collecting data) and reading experts' reports about pros and cons of the vehicles in which they are initially interested (considering various interpretations). Whereas some of the features of research are present, the detailed and rigorous processes associated with academic research are not all present. There are even differences in how research is explained in different universities and also within various levels of study at the same university. For example, an undergraduate student may be working on a paper "researching music therapy," while a graduate student might be "conducting a music therapy research study."

It is our view that many definitions of research are written from a methodological perspective and focus on the type of research or how it is conducted. This trend has been strongly influenced by the evidence-based practice movement and is based on a hierarchy of study types that ranks randomized controlled trials toward the top and interpretivist research near the bottom. This ordering was derived from medical and biological models. Although applying this model to music therapy might seem logical since we often work in medical contexts, the privileging of one type of research over another can be detrimental to our field. The slow movement from research constituting whatever might help to understand what works, to research being associated with a particular methodology, has been almost imperceptible to many of those within the movement.

However, not all explanations of research focus on methodology. Some intentionally include the vast research landscape. For example, the New Zealand Qualifying Authority (2014) provides a more holistic and encompassing definition developed in the context of arts-based research:

> [Research is] an original investigation undertaken in order to gain knowledge and understanding, typically involving inquiry of an experimental or critical nature driven by hypothesis or intellectual positions capable of rigorous assessment. It is an independent, creative, cumulative, and often long-term activity conducted by people with specialist knowledge about the theories, methods and information concerning their field of inquiry. Its findings must be open to scrutiny and formal evaluation by others in the field and this may be achieved through publication or public presentation. (p. 11)

---

[2] As noted in the preface, we purposely use this phrasing to be inclusive of a range of gender identities. "They" and "their" move away from a binary of "her" or "his" and toward a possibility of multiple gender identifications.

Within the music therapy field, Kenneth Bruscia (2014) has provided a concise but similarly inclusive explanation of research as "a systematic, self-monitored inquiry that leads to a discovery or new insight that, when documented and disseminated, contributes to or modifies existing knowledge or practice" (p. 21). Neither Bruscia's nor the New Zealand Qualifying Authority 's (2014) definition excludes any ways of knowing or inquiry, and both embrace the diversity of research questions and their associated methods. We believe it is vital for you to embrace a multiplicity of methods and designs in order to determine the most appropriate way to study your interest.

The definitions of research adopted by each academic will inevitably shape their teaching, and these definitions can be diverse. Whereas Bruscia's (2014) inclusive definition embraces multiple stances, this is not necessarily indicative of the most typical understandings in the field. In the United States, there has been a tendency toward developing restrictive understandings of what constitutes fundable or even real research. Gert Biesta (2007) suggested that research for the majority has come to imply "causal analysis by means of experimental research" (p. 3), which highlights the merits of the randomized controlled trial and negates the import of other designs. The overreliance and emphasis upon parallel group designs using quantitative data as the only type of research is disheartening, constraining, and congruent with our observations. There are still many questions to be answered about music therapy, and we believe it is critical to remain open to various ways of answering them.

Roles and Importance of Research

Because research represents a crucial and critical component of most allied health professions, it is embedded in most music therapy training programs around the globe. However, the specific requirements of your university will determine exactly what type of research project you need to conduct. For some, it may be carefully planning a project and providing a compelling rationale, but not actually collecting or analyzing data. For others, research training will also involve undertaking a small-scale study and the analysis of data to attain results. The variety in expectations is largely dictated by the emphasis of the program and the advising faculty member, as well as ethical considerations. A research-intensive university will often place greater emphasis on research, and therefore a greater proportion of time is spent on this part of training, while a teaching-focused university may have less of a research emphasis. In either case, the research component of your training can function as a gateway for the completion of a degree program and thus employment.

Beyond the end of your first research experience, there are other opportunities for continued research that also function as gateways for career advancement. Many undergraduate and master's students are required to complete a research project as a component of their degree program. To earn a PhD, a dissertation or thesis and accompanying oral examination or defense[3] is required in the United States. For academics working in research-intensive universities, research also functions as a gateway to tenure and promotion. To receive tenure and promotions at research-oriented institutions, academics are typically required to demonstrate their work is known nationally (for promotion to associate professor with tenure from assistant professor) and internationally (for promotion to full professor from associate professor). Small-scale research projects can also lead to the acquisition of grants to pursue larger and more complicated research projects. To acquire funding for large-scale projects, grant reviewers typically want to see an established record of publication and smaller projects in a related area, so they are certain the money they are allocating will be put to good use and result in a research product (i.e., research manuscript or publication) (see McFerran & Hunt, 2016). Thus, often regardless of one's standing or rank, research can function as a gateway for career advancement.

Within the health care professions, research can also lead to access to services for consumers. Music therapy, a health care profession with incredible breadth, is no different. In fact, since music therapy is such a small field (with approximately 8,000 board-certified music therapists in the United States), capable of meeting vast clinical objectives for a variety of service users, research may be perceived as even more crucial to the success of our field and our ability to serve consumers. The publication of a number of research projects in professional journals may prompt administrators to hire music therapists to provide services for their users and even encourage policy change. For example, Felicity Baker and Laurel Young (2016) noted that the systematic review and meta-analysis on the relationship between music therapy dose and response for people with mental health problems (Gold, Solli, Kruger, & Lie, 2009) influenced policy in Norway. However, in the contemporary era of budget cuts, limited resources, and scientific skepticism, it is important to be realistic about how research may influence policy. Additionally, certain types of research may have more influence on legislative policies than others. Nevertheless, without research demonstrating improved outcomes as a result of music therapy or that music therapy service users value and prefer music therapy, it might be difficult to argue for increased access to care.

The Process of Constructing a Research Question

Constructing a focused and elegant research question takes plenty of time and consideration. Although you may have many interesting ideas to investigate, it can be difficult to turn these into an intriguing and feasible question. We developed this book

---

[3] It is interesting—and perhaps unfortunate—that the term *defense* is frequently used to describe the oral exam of a dissertation or thesis. This term may inadvertently cause unnecessary anxiety, because it can be considered to have negative implications, when instead, the project and student should be celebrated for having completed a major task, milestone, and contribution to the literature.

to describe the various stages all researchers go through in writing research questions, although many of these are unconscious decisions. This guidebook makes those invisible processes visible and helps you to successively refine your interests so that your question is well thought through and clear. Therefore, each of the next four chapters represents a layer of influence that unconsciously and consciously shapes the way you conduct your research. In our minds, these layers of influence are nested within one another and move from your most internal and intriguing personal experiences at the center, out through an array of contextual influences. We believe that starting at the center and moving outward will help you create a unique research project that is internally motivating because it is based on your personal interests and experiences.

This book is purposely hands-on and includes chapter objectives to initiate thought processes and guide you toward synthesizing the factors that might impact your project and how you conceptualize it. While there are many books that outline the different types of research you can conduct, few texts help in the initial steps of the journey where a research question is realized. The following five chapters are designed to walk you through those first steps, up to the point of reaching a decision about what your research question and associated method might be. The layers are based on our own experiences of developing research projects, and they reflect many of the influences that have shaped our thinking. Your task is to discover what you can about your own research interests and the influences operating on you. We believe that, having done so, you will more easily generate a research question, identify your preferred method for investigating it, and eventually conduct the research. Based on our model (see Figure 1, p. 9), the final chapter is designed to support you to consider the myriad of factors that influence the way you write your research.

Layer 1: *Selecting your topic by identifying intriguing personal experiences with music, health, and well-being*
In Chapter 2, we will begin the process of selecting a topic based from your own intriguing personal experiences with music, health, and well-being. Since beginning researchers are usually inspired by events that have occurred as part of their music therapy practice or personal experiences related to music and health, becoming aware of and developing these ideas can lead to personalized and engaging topics. Becoming aware of and describing those experiences is therefore a crucial first step for generating broad ideas for your project. In this chapter, we will introduce examples of intriguing experiences based from our own research, and you will begin this process based on your interests and circumstances.

Layer 2: *Refining your question through awareness of your beliefs about music, health, and well-being*

In Chapter 3, we will start to refine your question by recognizing how your beliefs and values interact with your interests in music, health, and well-being. We explore how your choices can be shaped by your values, and we believe it is helpful to bring your beliefs and values into consciousness in order to make informed choices about how these values shape all your research decisions. As a therapist, these are important considerations in clinical practice, and as a researcher, these factors continue to influence what seems to be the "obvious" way to do research. In this chapter, we will explore those values, using various examples to reveal how values shape research trajectories.

Layer 3: *Aligning your method by identifying preferences for knowledge about music, health, and well-being*

In Chapter 4, you will begin to align your question and method by examining your preferences for knowledge. Since personal values intertwine with beliefs about what kinds of knowledge you think are important, one data type might seem "better" than another to you. For example, numbers might seem more convincing than words, or words more powerful than numbers. The university where a new researcher has studied shapes some of these beliefs, and within that, the beliefs of academic faculty members will inform what literature a new researcher reads, which, in turn, influences what appears to be the most valid or meaningful knowledge within the field. These influences are not separate; they weave together, often beneath consciousness, but they can be brought to conscious awareness. In this chapter, we will highlight the dominant methodologies shaping the music therapy discourse and encourage you to be creative in considering how to conceptualize and conduct your research projects.

Layer 4: *Considering the logistics by working with contextual influences that shape research about music, health, and well-being*

In Chapter 5, we will consider the logistical aspects of your research by studying how various contexts can shape your question. Having considered the factors at each level of personal interest; beliefs about music, health, and well-being; and beliefs about knowledge, we propose that a further hidden layer of influence is contextual parameters. By this we mean the communities in which we research, including the organization where we gather our participants, the policies that shape the range of services they receive, and the countries and cultures that encompass us all. Although these are far distant from the internal and often unconscious beliefs that we began with, they still influence our decisions in ways that can be difficult to consciously perceive. In this chapter, we will start the process of refining the question and method based from contextual parameters so the question effectively communicates with the scholarly community.

In Chapter 6, we will synthesize material from the previous chapters and complete exercises based from the content of those chapters. In this chapter, you will develop an epoché, a purpose statement, and an intriguing and practical research question. You will also receive peer feedback on your question and provide feedback to your peers concerning their research questions.

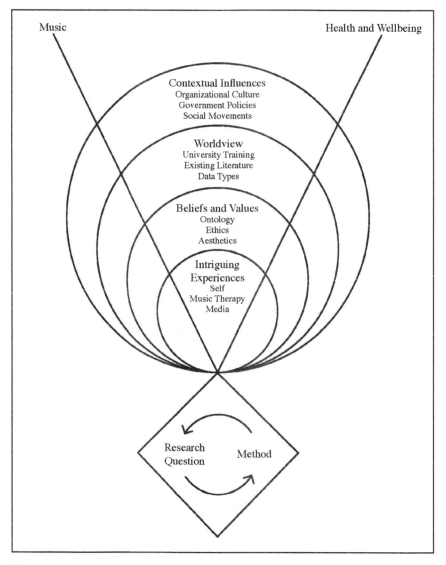

Figure 1

Chapter 2
Identifying Intriguing Topic Areas Stemming From Personal Experiences of Music, Health, and Well-being

---

Chapter Objectives

At the conclusion of this chapter, you will have:

1. Considered your experiences that led you to enter the music therapy profession

2. Reflected on things you have seen in music therapy practice that have intrigued you and piqued your curiosity

3. Contemplated the ways that music, health, and well-being are represented in the media, and how that may have influenced your topic area

---

Introduction

In this chapter, we describe how most research is informed by intriguing personal experiences a researcher has had with music, health, and well-being. This is entirely necessary, since research takes time and commitment and extends us beyond what we thought was possible. Therefore, your research needs to be grounded in a topic that engages and stimulates you. This sense of intrigue and curiosity then requires scaffolding, so that all the necessary practical structures are in place to support you as the project progresses. An advisor or graduate research class can provide the required scaffolding for developing initial ideas through thinking deeply about your topic, rather than leaping too quickly to a question and method. Although you will have encouragement from your peers and advisor, a research project is a journey that you take alone, synthesizing the existing literature, collecting data, and spending hours lost in those data, as well as months spent contemplating the possible meanings or explanations from what the data seem to be telling you. But this all begins with finding an intrinsically motivating topic. For that reason, this chapter focuses on being clear and conscious about why you have chosen a particular topic and how you should shape a research project that is aligned with motivations that will sustain you.

Although the degree of detail that is needed for planning a research project is far greater than what is required in music therapy practice, many of the skills we learn as therapists can be appropriated for the purposes of research. The most obvious overlap is our ability to listen to the unique stories participants tell us, whether that is through words, music, or numbers, since these characterize the data that inform music therapy investigations. Some people might even consider the information we regularly collect on our users' treatment progress to be data that, given Institutional Review Board (sometimes referred to as the Ethics Board or Human Subjects Protection) approval and appropriate consent, could be used for research purposes. But the skill we will focus on in this chapter is related to the processes that occur before data collection and that enhance your ability to observe the conscious and unconscious motivations that shape your topic selection. As music therapists, we develop our capacity to do this when learning how to understand the conscious and unconscious motivations of clients, patients, students, and others whom we meet in music therapy. You can use these same skills to explore and examine your own choice of topic in ways that add depth to your investigations, as well as focus and sustain your motivation if applied early in the research development process.

If you are able to understand the historical experiences that have shaped your interest in the topic you are investigating, this can provide you with stamina throughout the duration of the study. Personal reflection and analysis can illuminate a range of hidden factors that will influence your study, and as with all things in research, the detail is extremely important. Much as a psychodynamic therapist attempts to understand the unconscious dynamics of an encounter among themselves, a client, and the music, so do researchers benefit from examining the interaction among our past experiences of music, our music therapy practice, and our own health and well-being. The ways that you have seen and experienced music in your own life, both professionally and personally, provide the raw material from which your research interests are shaped. Some of these experiences will have been positive and inspiring, and others may have been particularly unsatisfying and frustrating. Since all experiences, both positive and negative, can be motivating factors in developing research ideas, understanding more about the personal experiences that shape your research is the focus of this chapter.

Layer 1: Identifying Your Own Intriguing Experiences

Many people pursue music therapy training because they personally have had a significant experience of music promoting health and well-being. This may have been your own experience, or you may have observed music therapy in action and been intrigued by how people were responding to the therapist and the therapeutic opportunities. Equally, it may have been something in the media that engaged your interest and made you curious about how or why it happened, or what it meant to the people involved. Whatever kind of intriguing experience you have had, these experiences remain in the back of your mind as you study and practice as a music therapist, and they can be a rich source for choosing the focus of your research study.

When reading the literature, you can sometimes hear how the writer has been inspired by their curiosity about a topic through the way they continue to investigate aspects of the same topic over years and decades. Finding this source of inspiration for yourself can provide you with a way of being similarly inspired, beginning with your first research project. This will be sustaining while you conceive the project, convince an Institutional Review Board that the study is ethically appropriate, recruit participants, collect and analyze data, begin the process of interpreting and writing the results, receive critique on your ideas from your supervisor or an external reviewer, and, finally, complete your research report.

Robert Duke (2010) describes intriguing experiences as those that fill you with curiosity and wonder. He argues that good research is inherently interesting because it explains something, even a little piece of something, that has been puzzling you. If the answer is already obvious, then it is not going to be interesting; it is not going to fill you with joy when you discover an explanation that might work, and it may not excite anybody else either. Research should come from a deep sense of intrigue, of wanting to explain something about a phenomenon. So, think of your own intriguing experiences with music, people you have met or read about (including yourself), and the interaction with well-being. We believe this is the most interesting way to begin, whether this is the first of many projects, or the only one you will do. It works best if you can find a topic that is personally meaningful, as Duke describes:

> All introductory courses in research should begin not with depersonalized descriptions of what we already know, but instead with a historical review of how inquisitive human beings came to identify interesting problems and how they advantageously employed the methods of research in solving them. (Duke, 2010, p. 213)

The following sections categorize the kinds of personal experiences of music, health, and well-being that many people have had, which could help you articulate a topic for your research project. These experiences are often related to people you have met through music therapy, since this is often the focus of music therapy studies, but the "participant"[1] may also be you or someone you know, or the experience may have occurred outside of music therapy. Since our experiences are unique, not all of the following categories will be relevant to every one of your topics, so it is likely that you will need to explore some more deeply than others.

It is common—and beneficial—to be torn between a number of good ideas. Take some time to examine each one of your ideas using the categories below (as well as categories in the other chapters), so you can ultimately decide which topic is most intriguing and practical and will sustain your excitement throughout the various phases of the investigation. By the conclusion of the chapter, you will be able to refine your topic

---

[1] We purposely use the term *participant* here to indicate that this person has willingly provided informed consent to participate in the research, and the researcher has approval to conduct research from their affiliated Institutional Review Board/Ethics Board.

choices to areas of interest, and we will then go on to explore the beliefs and values that shape your research question in the next chapter.

Factor 1A: Your Own Intriguing Experiences of Music, Health, and Well-being

Each of us brings a wealth of experience to our study of music therapy, and intriguing experiences may be why we chose to dedicate time and resources to studying the professional practice of music therapy. Music may have played a special role in supporting your own well-being. Since music therapists are all musicians, this might have been through your music practice on an instrument or voice. Perhaps music was where you found solace, or where you had the opportunity to express emotions that were too complex to describe using words. Perhaps being part of the school band saved you from isolation and you finally found a place where you belonged. Perhaps you received a lot of compliments for your playing and that helped you develop the confidence to do other things, or to recognize that you had something special to contribute. There are myriad ways that playing an instrument might have been connected to well-being in your own life, and, importantly, there might be something about your experience that you cannot explain. It is this aspect that you should consider focusing on and taking the time to explore now. What part of that experience has piqued your curiosity?

Intriguing experiences with music occur not just through music making, but also via music listening. Many people use music listening to enhance their well-being during difficult times, and you may have thought of music as your best friend, or your daily vitamin. Perhaps there were certain songs that spoke to you, or there were singers and players with whom you identified. It might have been a point of connection between you and your friends at school, or it might have been online musical connections that supported you through moments of adolescence when you did not feel understood by anyone in your daily life. Maybe you lay in bed and listened to music to help you relax and go to sleep, or maybe you chose music to make you cry and release emotions that were pent up inside. Once again, many aspects of these phenomena have already been explained by research, and your first task is to read the literature and understand what parts have been addressed. Through that process, you will likely find that questions remain unanswered. What part of your music listening remains fascinating to you, after all the moments of relying on music have passed, and what still does not make sense?

Perhaps it was not you that had the experience with music. Maybe it was someone in your family or one of your friends. Sometimes it is easier to think about the most intriguing aspects of music, health, and well-being when you were watching it happen, rather than feeling it happen. Perhaps you had a relative who presented with dementia and you were intrigued that they seemed most alive when you started singing rather than talking with them. Maybe one of your friends was struggling emotionally and relied on music to make them feel better in a way that you were unable to really understand. Perhaps you had a friend with multiple disabilities who seemed to come alive when you pushed their wheelchair up to the piano and encouraged them to strike the keys. It may have been the way that one of your parents relied on music for motivation to exercise or do housework. There are so many ways that you may have seen people you cared for using music to improve their well-being, but the question is, which one intrigues you?

For Kat, it was that music provided a way of expressing her identity during adolescence, as the following vignette illustrates.

When I was in my early teens, I lived in a very small town out on the edge of the desert that covers most of the Australian continent. It had been a great place to grow up as a child—swimming in the river, freely riding my bicycle everywhere, and being close to nature. But as I became an adolescent, the town began to feel small and constricting. Everyone knew me and there was nothing I could do without it being seen. There were plenty of ways to rebel, but there were fewer ways to stand out and explore what was unique about me. All the girls and boys my age played the same sport. I didn't know anyone whose parents were divorced, or who came from a different ethnic background, or who identified beyond a heteronormative sexual identity. I found it stifling and I longed for a way to be different.

Music was the thing that set me free. I was not the only person to play piano in my town, but I was the only student at my school who played saxophone. I carried my instrument proudly, and even though I was too scared to play in front of people, I used the saxophone case as a badge of my unique identity. In the 1980s, we listened to music on cassette tapes and the most portable medium for playing them was called a Walkman™. I used to carry my Walkman™ with me everywhere, with the headphones on my ears and, whenever possible, I would let my classical music tapes slip out of my bag. Nobody I knew was listening to Mozart, or Tchaikovsky, and these became another part of my unique identity that I wished to share with others.

This is one part of the reason that I have focused my research agenda on music and adolescents—a topic that has sustained me for the past 20 years. I still have many questions that I have not been able to answer, but I have managed to answer a few. I am still excited by this topic and I feel as though I could keep going for a long time yet before there is nothing left I need to know.

Factor 1B: Your Intriguing Experiences of Music Therapy

Since beginning your music therapy studies, you have had opportunities to observe music therapy being practiced by qualified music therapists and perhaps to begin facilitating sessions yourself. For many students, these experiences inspire a wide range of questions as you try to understand why the music therapist made certain decisions and acted in particular ways. Many of these questions are clinical and may not be the basis of a research project, but some of them will have the substance required for research. For example, a clinical question might be related to why the music therapist used that music therapy technique with that person, whereas a research question might consider why the music therapist used certain approaches with certain clients. Why might the therapist think it is effective? What do the participants say? What do their caregivers and family members say? What kinds of responses are observable? Does the benefit continue beyond the session? Each one of these subquestions is quite separate and requires a different approach to research, which we will discuss in subsequent chapters. The important task for now is to determine which question you find particularly intriguing.

In addition to the intriguing experiences you have when observing and facilitating music therapy sessions, there are special moments that you may observe that go far beyond your expectations. Music therapists are often benefactors of the empowering conditions created in sessions that lead to extraordinary breakthroughs for people. These moments cannot be predicted, since they are usually the result of a combination of factors that have come together in one moment to reveal an unexpected potential or powerful emotional response. Moreover, these moments in music therapy are difficult to forget, and they sustain you clinically. Many researchers have been inspired to pursue a particular research line in the hope that they will better understand these moments and have them occur more often for the people with whom we work.

Mike had one of these moments when working as a full-time clinician in adult mental health, as described in the following vignette.

After completing my master's degree, I wanted to gain additional clinical experience with people in adult mental health inpatient settings. I felt this was a marginalized, disenfranchised, stigmatized, and poorly understood group, and I had always been drawn to working with them. Being a "guitar guy" and a huge classic-rock fan, I was able to musically relate to many patients[2] who were older than me. Despite not having had a personal experience of mental illness, I felt the music provided a bridge for our interactions. I always enjoyed connecting with others musically, regardless of whether it was active music making or discussing music.

In this context, I was conducting biweekly group-based music therapy with adult inpatients on an acute care mental health unit. I had one particular patient whose progress was a bit slower, and he had attended numerous sessions with me. However, he never spoke during our sessions, regardless of the music therapy intervention I was using or the clinical objective I was targeting. Moreover, he never took his eyes off me, regardless of who was speaking in the session. He seemed to stare at me without blinking, which—to

_____

[2] We are purposely using the word *patients* here, as the context was an inpatient health hospital setting.

be perfectly honest—made me a bit uneasy. I was reluctant to try to verbally engage him in the group-based dialogue, as my clinical intuition told me that he did not want me to interact with him within the group music therapy sessions. He kept attending sessions and, although providing opportunities for him to actively participate, I did not pressure him to engage verbally or musically, figuring that he would make that decision when he was ready.

At the conclusion of one session, however, he approached me directly. He offered his hand in a handshake, looked me in the eyes, and told me he was being discharged from the hospital later that day. He thanked me for the music therapy sessions, saying, "Your sessions are the reason I'm getting out [of the hospital]. You have been the single most important and helpful part of my stay here and I'd like to thank you." As you might imagine, this caught me completely off guard.

I processed these interactions for next few weeks and engaged in supervision with my colleagues about this happening. Clearly, music therapy had a constructive effect on this patient. But, based on his observable behaviors, I did not think I was having a positive impact. This made me question the idea of verbal interaction within group music therapy sessions. Obviously, no person should ever be forced to verbally participate or interact in music therapy. From the experience with this patient, it seemed that just being in the sessions had helped. As I had always enjoyed social learning theories, I conjectured that this may be vicarious learning at its finest. This made me question how verbal interaction might relate to perceived helpfulness within group-based music therapy. Moreover, it made me question how accurate my observations of overt behaviors were, as I was clearly misperceiving the therapeutic alliance and the impact the sessions were having on this patient.

This encounter—and many years of pondering it—eventually led to a research study. In this project, I compared the frequencies and types of verbalizations people on an acute care mental health unit made during group-based music therapy with verbalizations made in group-based non-music therapy sessions (Silverman, 2009).

Factor 1C: Intriguing Media Representations of Music, Health, and Well-being

It is not uncommon to see extraordinary stories in the media of how music has changed people's lives[3]. You may have seen a video on YouTube or television, or read about an experience in print form. At the time we are writing this text, multiple videos are circulating on YouTube that capture an individual who is initially passive or unhappy or

---

[3] We consider a person's community as part of the term *media* in today's digital and increasingly connected age.

inactive and then becomes highly engaged and animated when music is introduced. One video begins with a baby sitting in a chair, staring at their mother, looking content. As the mother begins to sing, a range of emotions passes over the child's face. First, there is a look of excitement to hear the melodious voice; then, coinciding with a lyrical change that begins to describe grief and loss, the baby's face begins to crumple. Tears swell in the child's eyes and within moments sobs erupt. The mother continues to sing, assumedly to allow the viewer to see just how distressed the child is, and then finishes abruptly, gathers the child in her arms, and easily comforts her child while they both return rapidly to a contented state. This video raises a number of intriguing questions about the relationship between music and emotions and perhaps why some individuals are more sensitive to music than others. Some people might be intrigued about which musical element was the most powerful variable (i.e., the melody, tone, or tempo). Others might have questions about how music enhances the emotional quality of the relationship between caregiver and child. There are many ways your mind might be captured and your attention sustained by a short YouTube clip like this one. Your task is to delve into the particular aspects that you wish to focus on, before we take that idea into the subsequent chapters for further consideration.

Before there was YouTube, movies were (and still are) a popular forum for stimulating ideas about how music interacts with health and well-being. Awakenings (Sacks, 1973) is a book-turned-film that captures one fascinating phenomenon of how older people with neurological impairments can be "brought to life" by the introduction of music, among other things. Many aspects of the older people's responses within Awakenings are familiar to music therapists, as people who have been unresponsive for a number of years stand up and dance when music from their past is played. Others who have not spoken in years begin to sing when a particular tune comes on the radio, shocking all those around them. This is an intriguing occurrence, particularly to those who have not experienced it before, and this particular phenomenon has certainly caught the attention of researchers over time. As a result, music has played an integral role in the emerging field of neuroscience, because it provides a fascinating variable for testing hypotheses about how the brain works overall, as well as how music works specifically. Why can some people sing but not talk? What is it about the music that inspires this reaction? What is the context in which this phenomenon is most likely to occur? What does it feel like for those who are experiencing it?

Many of the ideas inspired by media representations could be classified as music psychology studies, rather than music therapy research. The difference between these two disciplines is porous, since music therapists often undertake music psychology studies because they are curious to better understand a phenomenon that influences music therapy practice, even though the studies do not directly examine music therapy. Some music therapy researchers may call these "basic" music therapy studies rather than music psychology studies, because they examine the foundations underneath the field. On the other hand, some music psychologists may call music therapy studies "applied" music psychology. Any of these interpretations can be correct, and it is simply a matter of respecting the context in which the research is conducted, particularly the discipline of the researcher. For your initial music therapy research project, your advisor's opinion of what type of research you are conducting—and how to appropriately label this project—is probably the most relevant.

Kat has completed a number of studies that have been published in music psychology journals, and the following is an example.

After I had conducted a number of investigations with bereaved adolescents, I began to think about how the knowledge could be made available to a wider audience, since many teenagers do not have access to music therapy. My research findings were useful for music therapists, but I thought they might be equally useful for young people who were grieving at home, alone in their rooms, and who had no access to support. I realized that investigating music therapy groups was one stream of research, but I also wanted to conduct research with teenagers who used music in their everyday lives, without a therapist. The knowledge generated could then be preventative as well as helpful during times of crisis.

To design a study for teenagers more generally, I needed to look at a broader set of literature and this involved reading in music sociology and music psychology. I needed to identify what questions had already been answered in a satisfying way and to carefully determine what I could best contribute. The result was a focus on young people in schools who may be struggling with depression but who were not receiving support. This made me think about how music could help prevent depression if introduced early enough and if strategies that were informed by music therapy principles could be made available to young people to try at home. I began to focus on music listening as a result and have since published in journals such as *Musicae Scientiae* (a music psychology journal) and *Youth Studies* (a sociology journal). Each journal also has different methodological expectations, so I carefully choose where my research fits best before submitting the manuscript for publication consideration.

Conclusion

Research is a highly personalized endeavor that ideally stems from the researcher's unique interests. These interests are usually informed by past experiences related to intersections among music, health, and well-being and may constitute our primary motivators when choosing general research topics. In our experiences at this stage of the research process, it is helpful to initially have multiple topic areas. It is then critical to engage with the literature to learn what is already known and what questions have already been answered. Although it may be tempting, it is not recommended to formulate research questions at this point. Rather, keep your primary interests in mind and remain open to different ideas concerning these interest areas. During the ensuing chapters, we will further refine, deconstruct, analyze, and narrow these areas. Based on the application of the nested layers to your interests, you will be able to choose a project that is most intriguing and practical.

Chapter 3
Recognizing How Beliefs and Values About
Music, Health, and Well-being Shape Your Research

Chapter Objectives

At the conclusion of this chapter, you will have:

1. Explored how factors such as ontology, ethics, and aesthetics shape your research interests

2. Considered how your values concerning music, health, and well-being impact your research interests

3. Recognized pre-existing assumptions that influence your research interests

---

Introduction

By the end of this chapter, you should have a richer understanding of how your beliefs and values about music, health, and well-being shape your research. In the previous chapter, we encouraged you to identify a topic to explore that is related to meaningful, personal experiences, and in the next chapter, we will help you explore what types of knowledge you consider most valuable in order to decide on your method. By the conclusion of the book, you should have developed an intriguing and feasible research question based on these factors.

In Chapter 2, you drew on your expertise as a therapist-in-training to explore how personal experiences with music, health, and well-being have influenced the topics in which you are interested. This chapter follows a similar process but focuses on a layer that has been explored by philosophers more than therapists. These topics are often discussed under the label of metaphysics or philosophy of science.[1] Although initially it may be difficult

---

[1] Metaphysics is often described as the branch of philosophy that addresses questions about reality and/or existence, in that it answers the question of "What is?" It can be traced back to Aristotle's work on the causes and principles of being, and his writing provides an early example of philosophical grappling with such issues. Even Ruud (2005) provides an overview of a number of approaches to music therapy research through the lens of philosophy of science in the second edition of *Music Therapy Research* (Wheeler, 2005), including positivism, phenomenology, hermeneutics, critical theory, systems theories, semiotics and structuralism, and postmodern currents.

to understand why philosophy is relevant to applied music therapy research, we believe the connection is important. This is seen in the roots of the word *philosophy*, which can be traced to "philo" = love, and "sophos" = wisdom. We believe the love of wisdom, and your desire to acquire it, will be an important part of what sustains your interest and energy throughout the research process once you have identified a topic area that intrigues you. When you conduct research, you are seeking wisdom about a topic that intrigues you, and this can be exciting!

The relevance of philosophy runs deeper than the root meaning of the word, however. Since philosophers explore the meaning of life, they have identified ways of exploring how we make meaning of life experience, just as therapists have learned ways to explore the psyche. This means you can learn how to examine your own beliefs and values from their approaches to ensure that your research question is captivating and intrinsically motivating. A number of philosophical ideas have been actualized into strategies for delving beneath research and exploring the beliefs and values that underlie decision making in research.[2]

One strategy used for this purpose within music therapy research has been the creation of an epoché. Examples of epochés can be found in the work of music therapists who have used phenomenological approaches in their research.[3] An epoché is another ancient Greek term that means suspending judgments in order to freely investigate

---

[2] Hermeneutic researchers work with the idea of acknowledging our prejudices, although it is described somewhat differently. Hermeneutic insights are those that become visible when the researcher reads between the lines, or tries to understand the subtext of written material rather than what is plainly visible. Becoming more conscious of our "nonproductive prejudices" (as suggested by Gadamer) or our presuppositions about a phenomenon (described by Heidegger as the "forestructures of understanding") — both of which are compared in a reasonably accessible way by Lawrence Schmidt (2016) — should allow you to clarify the focus of your investigation. If you desire, you could adopt a critical stance and be more suspicious and less accepting during this process. For example, critical hermeneutic researchers aim to remove the mask and expose the beliefs and values that are embedded in the language being studied, particularly those aspects that benefit dominant players at the expense of others.

[3] Writing an epoché is a technique from phenomenology that has been used by some interpretivist music therapy researchers to identify influences that might otherwise compromise their ability to describe the phenomenon as experienced by the research informants (see Nancy Jackson, 2016). Giorgi's (1997) notion of "bracketing one's biases" serves a similar purpose, although it is noteworthy that he used the term in its mathematical sense, where particular ideas/numbers are bracketed together but still included in the calculation (see Finlay, 2009, for further explanation). According to Giorgi, by acknowledging and bringing together our assumptions and biases about a phenomenon, we are better able to focus on what can be learned about the experience itself (that which is outside the brackets), alongside that which we would expect to see (inside the brackets).

a phenomenon. The processes underlying the epoché may vary but usually involve identifying your *a priori* assumptions about what the research results will constitute. In the following sections, we will ask you to work through a similar process by thinking about three different topics that influence how we write a research question, which we will describe as ontology, ethics, and aesthetics.

As you work toward narrowing your previously identified research interests, it will be helpful to explore your own ontological positions, your ethical stance, and your perspectives on the relationship among beauty, music, health, and well-being. By developing a reflexive[4] approach, you will sharpen your research interests, which will help you to refine key words so they more clearly convey your area of interest. The more you are able to identify and articulate your beliefs, the less you will find illogical contradictions embedded in your research question[5] and the easier it will be to develop a refined question and associated method.

If you need help to try to bring your own answers into consciousness, you can draw on some of the strategies that researchers use to write an epoché. The development of an epoché can begin when you write a bullet-point list or a story about what you assume will happen in the research project. When you engage in this process, you are actually writing a list of what you believe to be true. It is important to note that these points are not correct or incorrect, nor are they necessarily true for all people; they are simply your ideas, which will be valuable as you continue in the research process.

To illustrate this process of delving into your own beliefs and values, we present the reflections of "Sara" through a series of vignettes. This is not the story of any one person we have met, but we have generated these vignettes based on our shared experiences of supervising new researchers. Sara's story was written in response to a series of questions we designed to prompt reflections on beliefs and values about research. Our aim is that you will write your own story in answer to these questions and that this story will reveal your beliefs and values in relation to ontology, ethics, and aesthetics.

---

[4] The word *reflexive* is used in research to encompass a continual evaluation of subjective responses, intersubjective dynamics, and the research process itself (Finlay, 2002). This is beneficial at all stages of the research process, including the development of the research question (Guillemin & Gillam, 2004). Within music therapy, Brynjulf Stige, Kirsti Malterud, and Torjus Midtgarden (2009) have explored the value of reflexivity in articulating the questions that motivate our research, and they recommend that we evaluate the legitimacy and relevance of those questions when determining the quality of research.

[5] The result will be an inner unity that has internal logic, as Tina Koch (1995) describes it.

Layer 2: Beliefs and Values

Factor 2A: Ontology

Ontology is another word that is used in the philosophy of science to refer to beliefs about the nature of being and reality. Some people conceptualize ontology as a part of metaphysics, along with theology and cosmology, whereas others describe ontology separately as being the study of reality and what exists.[6] James Hiller (2016) describes how ontological beliefs "shape" (p. 99) the types of research questions we generate, and he distinguishes between realist and idealist ontologies. Barbara Wheeler and Kenneth Bruscia (2016) introduce the distinction between objectivist researchers, who believe in a single reality, and interpretivist researchers, who believe there are multiple ways of constructing truth and reality based on each person's unique positioning, or experiences. Whatever words you use, these beliefs about the nature of reality have already shaped what you believe is important to explore through research. While the experiences that intrigued you provide a broad topic area for investigation, your fundamental beliefs about how music, health, and well-being interact shape the focus and specific kinds of research questions you will ask. Although it is not easy to explain what ontology is, for a therapist in training, it is comparatively simple to ask yourself questions that will help elucidate your own beliefs about what is important, and these illuminate your ontological position.

Even Ruud (2005) notes that ontological questions may seek to define the nature of a phenomenon. In order to begin investigating your own beliefs, one question he suggests you ask is, *What is music?* We can make that more specific to your topic area this way: *Why do you believe music is important for the people you have named in your topic?* The following vignette illustrates how "Sara" would answer this question.

---

[6] David Martin and Kimberley Loomis (2007) have written an interesting chapter for teachers about identifying their own philosophy of education, and they use the grouping of ontology, cosmology, and theology to depict Aristotle's understanding of metaphysics. They also highlight values, but do so under the heading of axiology, alongside ethics and aesthetics. While their categorizations are slightly different from the way we have organized this text, and different again from the work of James Hiller (2016) within music therapy, different approaches are quite common in philosophy, since it is not about black-and-white thinking with clear and simple answers. Philosophy encourages the contemplation of different approaches to meaning making, and therefore different ways of talking about our "love" of "wisdom."

Sara has always enjoyed interacting with infants and had the opportunity to observe a music therapist working in the neonatology unit during the first year of her training. She was moved by the intimacy of connection between the music therapist and the infant and this became her preferred topic for the research project. After reflecting on her beliefs about music, she decided that, for her, music is even more powerful than language. She believes that music is a form of connection that is available to people—and certainly newborns—despite cognitive limitations such as brain injury or profound intellectual disability. She believes that when people engage in music together, they connect more profoundly than when they talk about different topics. When she observes mothers and infants vocalizing together, she can see how powerful music is as a form of communication and it brings tears to her eyes to know that even hospitalized infants in isolettes are able to find some way of connecting to their parents. This seems incredibly important to her. As a result of this insight, Sara is able to refine her topic from the broad area of music therapists in neonatology, to focus on the use of vocalizing with infants hospitalized in the neonatal unit.

Another question that relates to ontology, which may help you refine the focus of your research question, is to ask yourself: *What do I believe therapy is in this project?* It may be easier to answer a more tangible question, such as, *What is the role of a music therapist in this specific context with these people?*

As Sara attempts to become more conscious of her own beliefs about the role of the therapist, she thinks about what she has read in the music therapy literature. One observation she had was that there seem to be two main types of practice for working with infants. The first involves the music therapist working directly with the baby, and the second is focused on working with the caregivers of the baby. She recognizes that she feels torn about this divide in practice and becomes aware that this emotional response probably means it relates to her beliefs. She knows that when she eventually works in a neonatal unit, she wants to sing with the infants themselves, since this opportunity for deep connection is what has intrigued her from the beginning. On the other hand, based on her experience of the relationship with her own parents, as well as published literature indicating the importance of caregiver bonding, she fundamentally believes that caregivers are the most significant influence on the life of a baby. This makes her wonder about what form of practice she actually wants to investigate. She hopes that it will be possible to include both forms of practice in her future work but realizes that refining her research interest will require her to choose one of these for now.

As Sara is beginning to understand, many more questions are hidden within these two overarching questions: *What is music?* and *What is therapy?* The answers to these questions are shaped by a range of factors, including, but not limited to, your cultural memberships, privileges, relationships, and education. It may be worth trying to articulate what other questions could help you explore your ontological positions and refine your topics. The more time you spend reflecting on these positions, the better you will understand how your beliefs about music, health, and well-being influence your thoughts and actions as a music therapy researcher.

Factor 2B: Ethics

In this chapter, we are using the term *ethics* in a philosophical sense, which is sometimes called *morality* within the philosophy of science. Morality is similar to ethics in practice but refers to the theory about what is right and good. This is related (but different) to your professional obligation to practice in ways that are congruent with ethical guidelines. Ethical guidelines are rules that clearly delineate what is unacceptable—such as withholding services from people because of prejudice or developing personal relationships in ways that could compromise your professional ability to provide service. Ethical guidelines for practice relate directly to professional behaviors and boundaries, providing specific rules to guide decisions about that behavior. In this chapter, we focus on ethics in research as more closely related to the action of morality, which might involve your beliefs about what constitutes a *life well-lived*.

When it comes to exploring how your individual ethics shape a research topic area into a research question, it is useful to consider what practices you believe are "right and just" in the topic area you have identified. This involves focusing on the values you hold about how music therapy *should* be practiced and what you believe is "right and just" for the people who engage in music therapy. You will need to think beyond what is easy and feasible and reflect deeply on how you believe a research topic *should* be investigated.

One ethical question that all researchers are required to address is: *What are the rights of the people participating in our research?* Statements on ethical conduct in human research exist to emphasize the universal rights of all people involved in research. These include the right to refuse to participate without being penalized through a withdrawal of services or privileges. Another universal right that has been acknowledged after decades of deceit in research is to know how the obtained data will be used and what the purpose of the research is, unless a special case is made.[7] These are considered to be fundamental human rights in relation to research and all investigators must demonstrate how they will ensure that these are not violated.

The universal rights of the participants in our research are primary and inescapable and have been described in a range of music therapy texts.[8] In addition, to explore ethical questions that help us refine the detail of our topics in music therapy research, it may be pertinent to consider a more specific question, such as, *What do you believe is the "right and just" way of being a music therapist in the context of your research topic?*

---

[7] Although rare in the music therapy literature, some perception-based research necessarily involves deceiving participants in an attempt to eliminate potential biases and attain genuine data.

[8] All ethics documents are developed with a sensitivity to the local context, where different customs and traditions prevail. A number of music therapy authors have generated texts that consider a range of ethical considerations in their countries, including Dileo (2000) and Tsiris, Farrant, and Pavlicevic (2014).

Sara began to conceptualize her decision about whether to focus on the interaction between the music therapist and baby or the music therapist and parent as a personal ethical dilemma. She did not feel that any harm would be done to the baby if one approach were adopted over the other. However, she did recognize this question came from different beliefs about what was best for the baby at a critical moment of life. Without actual lived experience of being a parent or caregiver, Sara felt it was too hard for her to decide, so she raised the question in class and asked other music therapy students to describe their opinions so she could explore it further by considering diverse perspectives. Not surprisingly, the class was divided. Some people were defensive about the suggestion that a music therapist who chose to work directly with an infant might somehow be selfish. They felt the baby had the right to have a professionally shaped interaction with another adult using music. Others advocated for the rights of the caregivers to have the most intimate interactions with the baby and pointed to the vulnerability of their mental health, which could then also be linked to the mental health and development of the baby.

Another question that may help you reflect on your research topic area relates to your ethical stance on health and well-being. What you believe about health and well-being influences the kinds of services you argue people should have access to, and what purpose a music therapist serves. Therefore, another ethical question to consider might be: *What is the "right and just" type of service for a music therapist to provide based on the health and well-being needs of people in this context?*

Sara was now even more confused about the best focus for her research. She was slightly more aligned with focusing on the rights of the caregivers to have access to services that would enhance their relationship with their baby. However, this was mostly in order to do no harm—she did not want to advocate for anything that might make them feel left out or not musically competent enough to sing with their own baby once they had heard her singing. Although Sara was more easily able to consider what she thought could be wrong, she felt less clear about what might be right. As she reflected on her beliefs about the health and well-being needs of babies in the neonatal unit, she kept returning to the research literature that showed how singing to babies seems to improve their neurological development. She knew that working with the parents might mean the baby received less direct singing until she had been successful in encouraging the parents to sing more. Since the literature suggests that every day is more important than the next in terms of neurological development, she decided that the priority for her research would be investigating the music therapist singing to the baby. She also decided that in practice she would use this strategy only if caregivers were uncomfortable with singing themselves. She felt comfortable with this decision and understood her own beliefs more thoroughly as a result.

Another way of exploring ethical questions about rights to access music therapy services is to explore the opposite possibility. For example, you could consider what might happen if music therapy services were withheld for the purposes of research. If you place value on the benefits of music therapy, then it becomes more difficult to justify research conditions that mean some people have access to music therapy while others do not. This particular ethical dilemma is often considered by members of Institutional Review Boards (IRBs) who approve research studies and decide whether the project being proposed is ethically acceptable. IRB committees will usually consider the question of beneficence and whether the results are likely to be significant enough to a larger group of people in a way that would justify a smaller group of people not receiving clinical services.[9] An ethical question that might help refine the focus of your research project might ask: *Is it "right and just" to ask a research question that will result in withholding music therapy services?*

Once Sara realized that she believed an infant had the right to access music therapy services in the most immediate way, she began to think about some of the studies she had read in the literature. A number of these studies had used research designs involving control conditions, where the experimental group received treatment as usual with the addition of music therapy and the control group received treatment as usual with the exception of music therapy. She was puzzled that her values appeared different from these esteemed researchers and returned to the literature to investigate the issue more thoroughly. She noticed that some of the studies had used a wait-list control, so that the infants in the control condition would eventually receive music therapy later in their hospitalizations. However, this did not address her belief that services should be provided as quickly as possible to promote neurological development. As she read further, Sara realized this was a fine line, since too much auditory stimulation early in the development of the baby was also considered to be a health hazard by some researchers. This led Sara to reconsider what she thought was ethical, and since she was no longer clear about her position on the urgency of service provision, she returned to her values about the importance of the caregiver–infant relationship.

---

[9] The members of IRBs often focus on methodological factors in order to protect participants. The methodological section of the research proposal/protocol is the most tangible part of an application for research, and some would argue that it is therefore the most objective aspect for ethical consideration by a committee. However, as we describe in the next chapter, this view is built on particular beliefs about what constitutes knowledge and therefore suggests methodological design is crucial to the establishment of what constitutes strong research and what does not. Unfortunately, this can lead some IRB members to believe that only one type of research has value, wherein the primary purpose of the IRB is to protect the research participants. Therefore, a distinction should be made between the ethical decisions of the researcher and the bureaucratic process of the IRB, which intersects with both the worldview (Chapter 4) and contextual influences (Chapter 5).

The topic of ethics and morality has never been considered a simple one, which is why entire branches of philosophy have developed to consider different positions. Although ethical guidelines exist, interpretation is always required and decisions are often made by a number of people who form an IRB in order to debate various possibilities and not just to reach a simple conclusion. Within the philosophy of science, ethics is often considered alongside the topic of aesthetics, since both are related to goodness and value.[10] Since music is such an important part of music therapy research, we consider aesthetics to be an important area for consideration.

Factor 2C: Aesthetics

Aesthetics is the branch of philosophy that is focused on beauty. Music therapists usually have a particular set of beliefs about the value of beauty in the context of our practice, which often encompasses non-traditional sounds and performances that may not be easily appreciated for their beauty outside of a therapeutic process.[11] A number of North American music therapy scholars have described their own beliefs about the importance of aesthetics, most notably Ken Aigen (2007; *In Defense of Beauty*), Carolyn Kenny (2006; *Music and Life in the Field of Play*), and Colin Lee (2003; *The Architecture of Aesthetic Music Therapy*). It is clear that their views on the importance of aesthetic qualities have influenced the decision making of these researchers, who have all privileged a focus on the aesthetics of the music therapy process in their research, rather than emphasizing the non-musical outcomes attached to participation in music therapy.

In the philosophy of science, the field of aesthetics focuses on exploring the value of beauty in research, but once again, aesthetics is not about making simple judgments of what is deemed to be beautiful. Instead, it is about how each person's beliefs about what is beautiful in research influence their decisions about the design of the project. This is doubly interesting in music therapy research, since our medium is an aesthetic and creative one, and we bring values about beauty in music as well as in research.

---

[10] Axiology is another important branch of the philosophy of science, although it tends to receive less attention than the "big three" of ontology, epistemology, and methodology. It usually refers to the study of what the researcher values in research, and how these values inform the development of the research aims. For the purposes of this chapter, we have used the more specific terms of *ethics* and *aesthetics*, but axiology may be seen as an alternative, or as a category that includes both these terms.

[11] This expansive view of beauty is congruent with the argument made by educational philosopher John Dewey about the false division between high and low art that has been created in modern societies. It is also closer to the original notion of aesthetics, as posed by the Greek philosophers, who conceived it as being closer to truth and goodness than to an objective, or even subjective, judgment of artistic quality. See the thought-provoking essay by Greek music therapist Giorgos Tsiris (2008) for further explanation.

As you consider your own values about beauty in relation to the topic area of your research, it may be helpful to think about what you believe is beautiful. For example, you could think about how the relationship among music, health, and well-being may be related to the quality of your own musical contributions as therapist. Since many people associate beautiful music with years of training and understanding about the complexities of music, you might ask the question: *Does it matter if the music I make is sophisticated?*

Sara had never really considered the quality of the music used in the studies of neurological development through music. Some of the studies she had read noted using familiar nursery rhymes, and others described a musical form of infant-directed speech, but she did not remember if one result led to neurological development better than the other, or whether any particular kind of music was what made the difference. As she reflected on this, she began to question whether something as musically simple as a nursery rhyme could really make a difference to the neural activation of an infant. These songs are intentionally simple, repetitive, and have a small melodic range. They rely on predictable harmonies and short phrases that reflect the pitches of conversation more than the great melodic contours favored by composers.

Sara began to consider that the beauty of the shared music making was not in the notes themselves, but in the responsiveness of the music therapist. Perhaps the aesthetic value was related to how the music could reflect the beauty of the growing relationship. She had read about the theory of communicative musicality[12] and this seemed to be a closer match to her own aesthetic values than following a treatment protocol in which the musical material was predetermined. She felt quite sure that this was not the basis of the neurological studies that would have conceived of music as being a controlled variable and therefore privileged the use of a consistent stimulus, or the same song. This helped to confirm that her focus should be on the caregiver–infant bonding.

Another way of considering the value of aesthetics in relation to your topic is to ponder whether you conceptualize beauty as more connected to the product or the process of music therapy. It may be easier to determine value in a project by focusing on whether there has been an increase in musical contributions by the participants in music therapy. This might mean a person is more expressive musically, or it might mean they produce more music through increased singing or playing. The focus might be on musical contributions *during* the process, or a comparison from the beginning to end of the series of sessions, or a comparison with a control condition that does not receive music. In any case, some form of aesthetic judgment will be called upon to decide what you consider to be a meaningful change, and this will relate in some way to beauty.

---

[12] Communicative musicality (Malloch & Trevarthen, 2009) is the musical exchange within human interaction. The theory of communicative musicality was developed from research demonstrating how communication between mothers and their infants demonstrated noticeable musical elements, including timing, rhythm, timbre, and gesture.

The challenges of deciding what is aesthetically valuable in music therapy research may partially explain why there seems to be less focus on this than on other types of processes and outcomes.[13] A question that might be useful for exploring what you believe is meaningful could focus on the musical contributions of the people in your study. Consider how you would answer the following: *What kind of change in the music would be meaningful?* The way you answer this question should be helpful for clarifying the focus of your research question.

When Sara reflected on her experiences of music therapy in the neonatal unit, she could clearly remember times when she was excited by the infant's response. She thought carefully about what that sounded like and realized that what she found beautiful was the qualities of the sounds. Sometimes those sounds were gentle and seemed to convey the beginnings of emotional recognition. Other times it was the sheer strength of the infant's sound and her belief that this was some kind of determination to be heard. Sara realized that she thought the sounds were beautiful when she interpreted them as meaningful. Then she wondered if it was because they really were meaningful that she found those particular sounds to be more beautiful than other times when the infant made a different kind of vocalization. She realized that the aesthetic was not the focus of her research question, but that the process itself of engaging musically with the infant was beautiful and needed to be included in the question.

Having already reflected on her beliefs and values about the relationship among music, health, and well-being in relation to her topic, Sara now reflected on her ideas. In drawing together her ideas, she was creating a kind of epoché, wherein she began to shape her research interests into a more specific focus. She took the following points into account:

- Shared musical vocalizing was most interesting to her.
- Caregivers vocalizing with their own infants was her preferred focus.
- She would provide the musical offering if the parents were not willing or able to do so themselves.
- Bonding was more important to her than brain development.
- She did not want to include a control group in the study.
- The musical complexity of the adult vocalizing was not important to her.
- The quality of the infant's music was not an outcome, but it was meaningful.

It seemed that the purpose of her study would be to explore caregivers' perspectives of the qualities of meaningful moments when vocalizing with their infants and supported by a music therapist.

---

[13] Lars Ole Bonde (2016) has commented on the fact that "disappointingly" (p. 106) few studies focus on music itself, neither studies that used music analysis nor other forms of music-focused research.

Conclusion

Just as Sara was able to identify a range of beliefs and values that led to having real clarity in what she would investigate in a research project, so can the same process work for you. The more reflection you do on your ontological position (beliefs about what you think is *really* happening), your ethical position (beliefs about what you think you *should* research), and aesthetic position (what you value as *truly* beautiful), the easier it will be to write your research question.

Taking the time to create an epoché can help you become aware of the unique lens through which you view the phenomenon under investigation. Then it is time to consider choices that will lead you into the next chapter and the decisions you will make about what method will help you to best answer your question. We believe it is vital that we become overtly aware of these choices and the factors that shape our decision making. This increasing awareness can reveal the internal processes that inform how we narrow research interests to practical questions and associated methods.

Chapter 4
Understanding the Beliefs That Shape Our Preferences for Different Types of Research

---

Chapter Objectives

At the conclusion of this chapter, you will have:

1. Understood the alternative inquiry paradigms that different researchers align with in designing their studies

2. Clarified the differences between, and strengths of, interpretivist and objectivist approaches

3. Considered why you have a preference for certain types of data

4. Refined your understanding of how to select a method that aligns with your beliefs and interests

---

Introduction

As a musician, therapist, and student, you already have a range of experiences that you bring to research. As discussed in previous chapters, these influences shape how you perceive the world and intersections of music, health, and well-being. These experiences also impact your beliefs about knowledge and what you find to be the most compelling form of knowledge in a given circumstance. In this chapter, you will merge these experiences with an exploration of types of data and approaches to research to arrive at a tighter focus point for your research project.

The Great Debate

Historically, it has been possible to describe music therapy research as divided into two camps, or taking two sides of a great debate. These were initially labeled as *qualitative* and *quantitative*, terms that describe the different kinds of data that are collected by researchers on each side of the debate. In the latest edition of Barbara Wheeler and Kathleen Murphy's (2016) international textbook on music therapy research, the focus of the debate has changed from the types of data collected to naming the belief systems held by researchers in each camp—termed *interpretivist* (who would favor qualitative data) and *objectivist* (who would favor quantitative data) approaches. Arts-based research is also highlighted in the latest texts, pointing to an emerging and relevant field of research for music therapists.[1]

Helping you decide what type of data to use in your study is the focus of this chapter, and while we have chosen to focus on qualitative and quantitative data for the purposes of this text, please be aware that we support and advocate for a range of types of data, as well as mixing forms of data. Our decision is based partly on the focus of this book as an introduction to designing music therapy research questions, rather than a comprehensive account of how to use research methods to answer questions. In addition, although we each have our preferred paradigms based on factors presented throughout this text, we have both published, mentored, and advocated for interpretivist and objectivist research, as well as participatory, critical, and arts-based approaches. We believe all types of research have value and can lead to better understandings concerning if, how, and why music therapy might be helpful, best practice, and increased access to music therapy services.

Although multiple and changing labels about types of research can be confusing, they are also illuminating, since each term explains various research approaches using a slightly different focus. When you describe research, you will sometimes refer to the types of data, other times you will describe what will happen with the data, and sometimes you will refer to the belief systems behind the research process. It seems that researchers develop habits of using particular words as shortcuts or to point toward a group of concepts using only one part of the whole. For example, researchers may use the phrase "quantitative research" because it is familiar to people, even when they are talking about the entire design, not just the data type. This is further complicated by the different habits and traditions that exist in various countries and cultures, where some aspects of the investigation are considered more important than others. For example, Europeans seem more likely than Americans to have studied Western philosophy, and perhaps this explains why they tend to emphasize the belief systems that researchers adopt. In addition, a great deal of Western philosophy was written in Europe, and many of the ideas that seem complex and unfamiliar to those of us from other parts of the world might reflect cultural understandings that are familiar and reasonably straightforward to people who were born there. In contrast, there has been a longstanding focus on measuring outcomes in research in the United States that naturally aligns with collecting quantitative data. This might explain why language that focuses on data type—rather than paradigm or mode of inquiry—has become most common and less attention has been paid to other aspects of the research process. For a range of reasons, the words people choose to describe research may differ, and you

---

[1] Michael Viega and Michele Forinash (2016) provide an important chapter in the Wheeler and Murphy (2016) text that introduces these ideas to music therapy researchers. As they explain, many forms of arts-based approaches are relevant to consider, and all transcend the binary of qualitative and quantitative forms of data in different ways. It seems likely that transcending traditional interpretivist and objectivist approaches will become increasingly popular within music therapy research.

need to understand these differences. Therefore, the purpose of this chapter is to help you narrow, conceptualize, and then communicate various aspects related to the data of your proposed research project.

Paradigms

One way of organizing these ideas that has been popular with researchers in music therapy is Egon Guba and Yvonna Lincoln's (2005) notion of "alternative inquiry paradigms." The word *paradigm* was introduced into research by Thomas Kuhn,[2] who is responsible for the term *paradigm shift*, which points to a revolution in the ways that we see things and in the beliefs we hold about how to conduct strong science. An example of a paradigm shift in music therapy was the introduction of qualitative research projects in the 1990s, led by researchers such as Carolyn Kenny, Kenneth Bruscia, Michele Forinash, and Ken Aigen in North America. This might be described as a revolution because objective outcome measurement (i.e., an objectivist belief system using quantitative data) had been the dominant focus in the United States until that time and the introduction of an alternative paradigm shook the foundations of previously held beliefs. However, these ideas were gradually accepted and now it is normal to agree that there is more than one way to conduct strong research. As researchers, we were a part of this shift and readily believe and reinforce the value of various approaches to music therapy research, as seen in this chapter and throughout the text.

Rather than focusing only on qualitative and quantitative data types or interpretivist and objectivist belief systems, Lincoln, Lynham and Guba (2017) propose a matrix that outlines five different approaches (Positivism, Post-Positivism, Critical Theory, Constructivism, and Participatory) and then layers within each. They use three categories of basic beliefs from metaphysics (ontology, epistemology, and methodology) to highlight the differences across five inquiry paradigms. In the Table 4.1, we have condensed some ideas from the five columns of Lincoln et al.'s matrix[3] into two columns in order

---

[2] Kuhn's (1962) notion of paradigms was described in *The Structure of Scientific Revolutions*, where he explains that many major scientific advances are achieved when the field responds to a crisis in the current model of beliefs and a revolutionary model emerges, leading to a paradigm shift. In this sense, a paradigm is a set of beliefs that is shared by a particular scientific community and that dictate what kinds of research questions and methods are privileged in that field.

[3] In fact, Lincoln, Lynham, and Guba's (2017) matrix is beautiful in its complexity, and it has continued to evolve over a number of editions of the *Sage Handbook of Qualitative Research*. They have purposely avoided simplification into the binary of objectivism and interpretivism in order to illustrate the diverse belief systems that inform decisions made by researchers who are adopting a particular stance. Their discussion of paradigmatic controversies, contradictions, and confluences is an excellent introduction to the concepts we have briefly summarized here.

to illustrate the Great Debate that has been prominent in music therapy research. In addition to this understanding of two major approaches to music therapy research, we note again that participatory, critical, and arts-based approaches have been increasingly represented in the music therapy research literature. Although we highlight the two most common approaches in Table 4.1 because of our focus on introducing you to research in the context of your first project, we encourage you to explore and integrate ideas from the five inquiry paradigms as your research career evolves.

Table 4.1: *Words Commonly Used on Either Side of the Great Debate*

	Objectivist	Interpretivist
Paradigm	Positivism/Post-Positivism	Constructivism
Type of Researcher	Objectivist, positivist, post-positivist	Interpretivist, constructivist
Type of data	Quantitative, objective, observable	Qualitative, subjective, experienced
Ontology	Reality is fixed and measurable	Reality is dynamic and negotiated
Epistemology	Seeks facts about phenomenon to generalize from	Seeks meaning and understanding from participants' unique perspectives
Methodology	Experimental, primarily rely on quantitative data	Exploratory, primarily rely on qualitative data
Approach	Measure and test	Observe and interpret
Participants	Emphasis on large samples of participants in order to generalize; randomization encouraged	Emphasis on quality of understanding gathered from local informants with lived experience
Analysis	Generally deductive, using numerical comparisons and statistical inferences	Generally inductive, generating interpreted themes, categories and theories
Quality	Validity based on methodological choices	Demonstrated by reflexivity in interpretations of data
Reporting	Statistical analyses	Rich descriptions
Research questions	Narrow, focused	Broad, open

In the mid 1990s, American leaders in the interpretivist music therapy movement often suggested that researchers would identify with one of the paradigms over the other because each reflects an individual's belief system, which does not easily change.[4] However, many music therapists struggle with this division and enjoy collecting different forms of data to gain distinct perspectives on the topic they are investigating and on the people with whom they are working. It may be true that the way researchers analyze those data ultimately reflects more about their belief systems than the type of data, since separate researchers might collect the same data but will likely analyze it according to their beliefs. For example, Mike usually adopts an objectivist approach but has conducted a number of studies in which he has collected qualitative data. Because of his basic beliefs, he does not tend to emphasize the interpretive aspects of the analysis or reflect on how his opinions have shaped the categories he finds, but he enjoys qualitative data because they convey the unique voices of participants and their narratives. Similarly, Kat usually adopts an interpretivist approach but has collected quantitative data from surveys and self-report measures in a number of studies. Because of her increasingly critical worldview, she tends to emphasize findings that seem to contradict the researcher's expectations or are imbued with cultural assumptions, rather than accepting the objective results as accurate. In both these cases, our beliefs are more apparent in the analytic process than they are in the type of data we collect. You may also find it difficult to align with only one paradigm, but perhaps music therapy researchers are particularly flexible and willing to consider a range of different forms of knowledge, as the increasing interest in arts-based research suggests. We believe it is important to understand how your beliefs about what constitutes valuable knowledge leads you to particular choices of methods for any one research project. Whether that generalizes to all the research you conduct is a point for your own contemplation.

Psychotherapeutic approaches and orientations may also influence perspectives concerning the Great Debate. Theoretical perspectives concerning if, how, and why therapy may be effective can influence research questions and resultant modes of inquiry. For example, psychodynamically oriented clinicians and researchers study factors that are

---

[4] Kenneth Bruscia was particularly influential during this stage of research development and provided a number of documents that assisted in understanding the differences between quantitative and qualitative research, or different ways of knowing. His 1998 article concerning standards of integrity for qualitative music therapy research provided an explanation of equivalency in research standards that used a comparison between the two stances as a way of explaining and introducing approaches to music therapy research to "enlarge our constructions of the world and to find and create individual meanings therein" (p. 176). Additionally, Ken Aigen (1995) provided an early comparative overview of different methodological approaches in the first edition of the *Music Therapy Research* text. This helpful synthesis of approaches being used in music therapy research also seemed to be grounded in an assumption that researchers could identify with one, but not both, paradigms, since the differences between approaches were essentially in conflict with one another and assumedly could not easily be resolved within one individual.

typically difficult to quantify (such as awareness and insight), while cognitive behaviorally oriented clinicians and researchers tend to study observable, measurable, and replicable behaviors that can be captured with quantitative data (often within a prescribed number of sessions). Although cognitive behavioral researchers certainly are not precluded from conducting interpretivist research and psychodynamic researchers are not precluded from conducting objectivist research, these are not the typical tendencies.[5]

In this chapter, we will use ideas that have been associated with the notion of epistemology to work through the influence of your beliefs on choices of method, just as we used the notion of ontology to consider your research focus in Chapter 3. Epistemology is the branch of philosophy of science that considers the nature of knowledge and how we acquire it. As you begin to consider the different ways you form your beliefs about what is true and how you can acquire new knowledge, you may notice considerable differences across the paradigms. For example, if you align with an objectivist inquiry paradigm, you are likely to believe in logic and verifiable quantitative data. However, you may still accept that pure objectivity is difficult to achieve in research with people in real-world contexts and therefore may favor more flexible, post-positivist approaches. Your data sources would emphasize what can be repeated or compared and therefore would need to be carefully controlled so these patterns can be identified. Conversely, if you find yourself aligned with an interpretivist inquiry paradigm, you may naturally embrace the idea that every person has different experiences that make it difficult—if not impossible—to generalize, such as each member of a music therapy group experiencing idiosyncratic benefits from participation. Therefore, you would be interested in hearing the unique story described by each participant and choose to engage in open-ended conversations to collect data, rather than needing to ask the same questions in order to determine how similar the answers are.

While the differences in beliefs held by people who align with particular inquiry paradigms are interesting, it is important to recognize that these are socially created constructs, and not tangible objects.[6] We believe it is important for you to explore your beliefs, but also to recognize that divisions in research are social constructions and do not constitute facts. As such, these divisions have certain benefits but also dangers. This has been highlighted particularly well by critical and feminist researchers, who have expressed concern about the creation of needless and even dangerous binaries. This kind of reduction forces people to identify within overly simplistic constructions of sex and

---

[5] Munhall and Boyd (1993) noted that this factor can also be conceptualized as studying the *process* of the treatment (psychodynamic therapy via qualitative data) or the *product* of the treatment (cognitive behavioral therapy via quantitative data).

[6] Historically, these divisions have not even existed, and Brynjulf Stige and Roger Strand (2016) suggest that it was the introduction of the term *scientist* in 1833 that created the need for any divisions. They explain how thinkers prior to then had been inclined to canvass a range of approaches including philosophy, natural and social sciences, and even mathematics.

gender that are heteronormative, with distinct and disconnected ideas of masculine and feminine.[7] Although the implications of binary positions are perhaps less severe in music therapy research, concerns have been raised within the music therapy discourse about the simplistic and binary division that underpins the Great Debate. Since music therapy is both art and science as well as an internal experience and external expression, it does not fit easily into a single, all-encompassing model. Researchers, such as Carolyn Kenny (2006), highlight how arguments based on one set of ideas being superior to another therefore do not capture the breadth, depth, or complexity of either the profession or the discipline.

Clifford Madsen made reference to the conflict between research methodologies as long ago as 1974, noting the enduring conflict could be damaging to the music therapy discipline. Researchers who have considered their approaches as superior to others have sometimes placed limitations on what they consider to be good enough research to be published or even presented at conferences. In this way, some forms of knowledge have been shut down, while others have been able to flourish. Our position is that it can be healthy for research methods to be in opposition to one another, since debate can benefit science and facilitate the development of new knowledge. Rather than hoping everyone might agree, we believe that agreeing to disagree and holding respectful conversations that honor the different aspects of others' work is important. Focusing exclusively on the aspects of a colleague's work that are different from your own in an unconstructive manner is unproductive and often results in a negative research attitude. Although there are undoubtedly differences in beliefs that can be difficult to manage, ultimately, we can aspire toward celebrating these differences to allow us to have a more holistic understanding of the rich intricacies of our field.

Mixed Methods

Within the Great (binary) Debate, mixed methods can sometimes be conceptualized as an olive branch, demonstrating how both qualitative and quantitative data can be considered as worthy. This approach has sometimes been useful in maintaining peace and avoiding arguments, but it can also reinforce binary thinking, since it is based on assumptions about the purpose and functional properties of qualitative and quantitative data. Indeed, Bryman (2007) noted that not all those who favor mixed methods are alike and introduced a pair of words to categorize mixed methods researchers as either

---

[7] This is a broad field of research and theorizing, to which a number of North American music therapy scholars have contributed, including Sue Hadley and Sue Baines. At the core of this particular critique of "binary'" positions is the idea that putting people into one of two categories creates unnecessary division and dangerous simplifications. It reduces people to one dimension of their intersecting identities—the most common being biological sex or skin color. Nina Lykke's *Feminist Studies: A Guide to Intersectional Theory, Methodology and Writing* (2010) provides a useful historical account that leads to an explanation of current perspectives on this topic.

particularistic or *universalistic*.[8] The "father" of mixed methods research, John Creswell, has developed a range of mixed methods designs that explicitly acknowledge which approach is being privileged within a particular study (Creswell & Plano Clark, 2011), once again emphasizing the more objective or subjective inclinations of researchers. This distinction can be telling. For example, if you choose to begin by collecting qualitative data that then informs how quantitative data are collected (i.e., an exploratory sequential design), you may be emphasizing the value of subjective perspectives. If you begin by collecting quantitative data and then use qualitative data to help understand the results (i.e., an explanatory sequential design), you may be emphasizing objective knowledge.[9] Distinctions within mixed methods approaches are therefore critical and require you to understand the alternative inquiry paradigms and the difference between interpretivist and objectivist approaches.[10]

Because you are a beginning researcher designing your first project, we do not recommend using mixed methods inquiry. This caution is not because we do not believe in or support mixed methods. Rather, it is best to keep your research question focused on a single question when conducting your first project, since there is enough to learn in becoming familiar with one approach, let alone two. By definition, mixed methods studies have (at least) two research questions, with one question for the qualitative data strand and one for the quantitative data strand. Additionally, in true mixed methods studies, analyses of these data strands are mixed, and this typically requires a pre-existing understanding of how each works separately in order to amalgamate the strands. This level of research sophistication is challenging for any researcher and would certainly test anyone conducting their first research project.

Having outlined some of the key strengths and pitfalls of the Great Debate, it is now time for you to explore in more detail your own beliefs about what constitutes strong research. In the following sections, we highlight three factors that can be related to epistemological questions and that shape decisions about what kind of research method you might adopt. As with the previous chapter, we offer you an extended example of how "Mateo" has worked with his beliefs and worldview in order to come to a clear decision about the type of methods he will use in his research.

---

[8] According to Bryman (2007), if a researcher is trying to understand if, how, and when a novel intervention is effective in a certain context, mixed methods research might be best to understand both *if* (quantitative data via a between–group comparison) and *how* (qualitative data via interviews with research participants and interventionists).

[9] Creswell and Plano Clark (2011) also noted that some studies can emphasize and privilege certain data types by using capital letters, such as QUAL and quan versus qual and QUAN.

[10] Readers interested in mixed methods music therapy research can consult Bradt, Burns, and Creswell (2013). Additionally, Bradt (2015) provided publication guidelines for mixed methods music therapy research. For detailed information on mixed methods from a non-music therapy perspective, see Creswell and Plano Clark (2011).

Layer 3: Understanding Your Worldview

Factor 3A: University Training

One factor that shapes how you conceptualize your own research in music therapy is the academic training you have received. This is not a singular influence, since most of you have had numerous people involved in your academic training, including music therapy professors, people making conference presentations, research courses you participate in, peers, and clinical supervisors. All of the people you meet during training have the potential to shape what you find interesting and what you believe to be the active mechanisms of change within music therapy. The people who influence you do this in subtle as well as explicit ways: by the literature they assign for reading, the studies to which they refer, and even the practice theories they emphasize. For example, a music therapy student training in an academic setting that emphasizes psychodynamic theories may come to believe that the relationship between the client and therapist is the most crucial influence on whether there are likely to be beneficial therapeutic outcomes. This might then influence research interests toward focusing on the relationships among music, the client, and the therapist. Or it may suggest that comparing different music therapy methods is irrelevant because the relationship dynamics are the most important mechanism of change, and therefore it would be better to focus on only the process as experienced by the client. By contrast, a music therapy student in a behaviorally oriented program is likely more interested in observable and measurable differences that provide tangible evidence of change. They may therefore be enthusiastic about investigating when those changes occur more often, and what conditions seem to promote those behaviors better than others. In both cases, it is not necessarily the lectures on research *methods* that have influenced thinking. Rather, it is the emphasis of the program, as well as the knowledgeable individuals they meet while studying it, that have shaped their thinking. We are often unaware of these influences until they are made conscious to us.

Specific research training does, however, play a powerful role in how you conceptualize knowledge and how knowledge is derived. Every professor will have their own preferences, and since most academic music therapy programs are comprised of a small number of faculty, they are unlikely to span all the paradigmatic inquiry approaches mentioned earlier. The usual result is an emphasis on particular approaches to research, whether demonstrated through the number of lectures spent on specific methods or simply a greater enthusiasm being apparent for different topics. If the professor has a wealth of experience in collecting data through interviews and conducting interpretive analyses to reveal new knowledge, they will have richer examples to share in teaching that topic. If they have found statistically significant differences in a research line comparing participants who receive music therapy with those in a control condition, this may inspire their students to think they should also contribute to the evidence base in a similar manner. If the faculty member is a critical thinker, they will inevitably highlight the oppressive power structures that shape research in the field, and the research student will then be able to better conceptualize and articulate how some methods might disempower or disregard participants. Congruence with your advisor's preferred paradigm can be an advantage, and it would require a great deal of determination and independence to maintain a firm faith in alternative approaches to your advisor's when you are designing your first project as a student. But it is possible, although you may need to convince your advisor.

However, many students develop clinical and research interests that are similar and related to their mentors' interests. These interests may have been part of the reason you chose to study at a particular university, or they may have grown since gaining clinical experience. Your interests may have even evolved from pragmatically based decisions related to earning higher grades by adopting faculty views. On the other hand, you might prefer taking an alternative stance so you can challenge assumptions and establish yourself as an independent thinker. Or you may have firm views that are different from the dominant view in your university, which will inevitably be frustrating at times. This difference should not be problematic, since most academics strive to teach across a range of topics that are not their first preference. However, the influence of hidden factors can be difficult to understand, which is why we believe it is useful to consider them. You can start by asking yourself the question: *Does my training emphasize the value of internal experience or observable and measurable effects?* This can help to clarify why you might privilege one kind of data over another. The example of Mateo illustrates this point, as he reflects on his university and clinical training experiences and considers what kind of data are most valuable.

Mateo is a music therapist practicing in an adult inpatient oncology setting. He is also working toward a master's degree and is currently in the stage of narrowing the research topic for his thesis. He is interested in conducting research at his current medical facility where he has access to patients with cancer and the support of administrators and the interdisciplinary treatment team. Mateo's primary philosophical approach to working with his patients is psychodynamic and he uses clinical improvisation as his principal intervention. He learned this approach and corresponding music therapy technique[11] from both his academic advisor and supervising clinical internship director. After observing both of these mentors utilize the approach and intervention—and the corresponding beneficial results with patients—Mateo knew he wanted to study this topic further so he could better understand the processes and products of this form of music therapy practice.

Although Mateo was primarily influenced by his music therapy academic advisor and internship director, he was also impacted by a cognitive behavioral therapy (CBT) course he took during his master's coursework. He enrolled in the course to broaden his philosophical approaches, as he believed that if he relied too heavily on a singular approach, it might limit his therapeutic impact, because particular approaches might not be effective for all of his oncology clients. After taking the CBT course, Mateo began to merge aspects of cognitive behavioral therapy into his work. For example, he was able to incorporate cognitive reframing techniques when working with his patients to help them better understand their perceptions of their problems as well as resultant behaviors and emotions stemming from these cognitions. Additionally, through this course, Mateo felt better able to assess patients and develop observable and measurable treatment goals while using clinical improvisation as his intervention. Mateo now considers his approach eclectic, as he uses a variety of philosophical orientations with his patients, who are typically quite diverse and have changing needs resultant of the cancer and various treatments. Because of his eclectic orientation, Mateo has been struggling with what type of data he considers most powerful. He believes that interviews would be helpful for understanding the processes of practice, but he also thinks those processes result in measurable changes in people's lives. If that were the case, he could gather evidence of it and provide generalizable quantitative data.

Mateo's dilemma is familiar to many of us, not only in choosing an eclectic approach to practice, but in valuing both qualitative and quantitative data. As described above, we both have collected different types of data in our studies, sometimes even within mixed

---

[11] In the United States, it is common to refer to techniques and experiences as interventions, particularly in medically oriented contexts. In Australia, these might be called methods. From Norway, Randi Rolvsjord (2010) critiques the language of *intervention*, noting that the word is laden with a range of powerful associations, from the military to an expert model that assumes someone other than the client is responsible for change. Different words are used in different countries and contexts, but here we are using the term *technique* to refer to the musical actions taken by the music therapist as part of the therapeutic process.

method studies. But, ultimately, you need to decide what type of data you will collect for each study you conduct, beginning with the one you are contemplating now. Understanding whether you are more inclined to objectivism or interpretivism is a good place to start. Are you more convinced when you can see the ways that people have changed with your own eyes (which would lead to objectivism), or do you find people's descriptions of their internal experiences the most compelling (which would lead to interpretivism)? It is easier to make this decision if you focus on your research purpose and ask the question for this particular project, rather than try to reach a conclusion that is true for every diverse moment of your practice. It may be helpful to ask yourself the question: *What kind of data would I find most convincing for this study?*

Factor 3B: Existing Literature

As the content of the current literature should also influence how you conceive various aspects of your study, it is *imperative* to conduct a thorough literature review.[12] The work you read that has been conducted by academics beyond your own university has a powerful influence on what you believe is quality research, especially because it is published in books and journals, which confers a certain power and authority to it. Within that research literature, there will tend to be an emphasis on particular methods of research and data types. When renowned researchers in the field approach their projects in a certain way, this can influence what we believe is the "right" kind of data. For example, if all researchers investigating group music therapy work with adolescents are conducting interviews, then it seems almost inevitable that you should also conduct interviews. Alternately, if everyone is collecting data using validated tools before and after music therapy sessions, then it will seem likely this is the "best" way to proceed.

Although sometimes not explicitly stated, the author's beliefs about knowledge (i.e., the author's worldview) lie underneath each research article. One of the ways these beliefs are made apparent is in decisions about the kinds of data a researcher has collected. Their worldviews then influence the beliefs you form about knowledge as you read their papers and notice the types of data and the ways that data are used to reach conclusions or propose theories. Depending on your background and how closely aligned your professor's views are with the literature, you might find yourself either convinced or frustrated by the decisions described by authors. Perhaps because a particular type of data is most commonly collected, you are curious about what could be discovered if other researchers had approached the project differently. Or perhaps the literature is so convincing to read that you feel there is no choice about what types of data are most valuable, and therefore you do not question whether it is aligned with your own beliefs.

---

[12] Readers are encouraged to consult Elaine Abbott's (2016) chapter on conducting literature reviews, as the literature review constitutes an essential aspect of research.

If you take the opportunity to reflect upon your reactions to the literature, you can use what you discover as an indicator of your own beliefs. Whether you are convinced or curious about what is missing from the existing literature is one way of discerning your own beliefs about knowledge. This can help you become aware of what you value and believe in, which is certainly different for each person reading the literature. In the following vignette, Mateo attempts to navigate and discern influences from the existing literature.

As Mateo reflects on the adult oncology literature beyond music therapy, he is struck by an emphasis on physical outcomes for patients. In particular, he notices that fatigue is frequently the primary complaint of cancer patients. The fatigue is often a side effect of the medically oriented treatments. Mateo's primary aim was usually related to internal coping processes associated with having cancer, and he has never explicitly focused on fatigue in his sessions. Both the psychodynamic and cognitive behavioral approaches he adopted have been focused on internal growth, change, and coping in response to illness, not targeting physical results of the illness or the side effects of medical treatments.

Mateo returns to the medical oncology literature and is confronted by the lack of emphasis on the aims that he considers to be most important. Since he really wants to conduct research that his hospital colleagues will appreciate, he begins to wonder how improved coping with cancer might lead to a reduction in fatigue. If he could make a logical argument about the relationship between these two factors, he might be able to collect data on fatigue but still remain true to his usual aims for music therapy.

Once again, the dilemma Mateo faces may feel familiar. Music therapists often focus on the psychosocial impacts of therapy, but also assume that improvement in this domain will translate to improvements in other domains, such as reduced fatigue. While this may be true, it is risky to make leaps in understanding or assumptions within a research project. During the scope of a single isolated research study, it is often more practical to design an investigation that directly links your research purpose with the type of data that you will collect. If Mateo applies this idea, he therefore has at least two possibilities to consider.

It is clear from the literature that an improvement in levels of fatigue would be valuable for oncology patients. Having become convinced of this from the existing literature, Mateo decides to focus his research on fatigue. He attempts to integrate his improvisatory approach to music therapy with his interest in targeting fatigue in patients with cancer, and he generates the following statement: *The purpose of this study is to understand which music therapy approach might result in the greatest improvements in fatigue levels for adult patients with cancer in a hospital setting.*

Mateo feels convinced that he observes a reduction in fatigue after he has used improvisation as his primary method. This idea is justified by literature he has read, which suggests, somewhat counter-intuitively, that expending energy (in this case, actively playing instruments during therapeutic improvisation) is one of the ways to reduce fatigue. However, he has also noted that working with a cognitive behavioral approach using songwriting does not seem to impact fatigue, although it has other benefits (including coping and self-expression). Since improvisation requires more active and physical engagement than the songwriting interventions, he wonders if the active physical engagement in clinical improvisation may be the explanatory factor for the reduction of fatigue.

As Mateo turns his attention to fatigue-based literature within oncology, he finds different established psychometric instruments that rely largely on the self-report of patients describing their internal states. After looking more closely at the methods being used in these studies, Mateo recognizes that self-report data are presented in two ways: (1) patients freely expressing their own opinions within interviews (i.e., qualitative data), or (2) patients answering predetermined questions in surveys that have numerical values (i.e., quantitative data). He is impressed by how the surveys have been validated with large samples of people in previous studies, and he imagines that his results will be more convincing for his hospital administrators if he were to use an established measurement tool. His advisors agree that it is best to use existing measures (rather than creating a new instrument or using a single Likert-type scale) in a medical context. They suggest that a pre- and posttest design will be the most useful approach if his hypothesis is that music therapy in the form of clinical improvisation will improve fatigue.

Both of these options reflect Mateo's objectivist worldview, which has been partly shaped by his reading of the literature. In his reading, he is regularly drawn toward outcomes that can be measured; this is one way of identifying that his preferred inquiry paradigm is objectivism. This is also influenced by the context of the dominant beliefs about knowledge held in his workplace (discussed in the next chapter), as well as his own beliefs about how music and therapy work together (discussed in the previous chapter), and the influence of his music therapy training (discussed above). But the literature is undoubtedly another one of the many interacting factors that shape our beliefs about what kinds of knowledge are most valuable.

The example of Mateo highlights the possibility of holding seemingly opposing beliefs about approaches to practice (that might be considered within your ontological stance) and approaches to research (that we are labeling your epistemological stance). In both of the options in the example above, Mateo is choosing to focus on outcomes from participation in music therapy rather than processes of music therapy. This is despite his preference for process-driven improvisation and his emphasis on the therapeutic relationship within his practice. These views are not contradictory, since what you consider to be strong research can sometimes differ from expert clinical practice. We have intentionally highlighted this possibility since people can sometimes make assumptions about a music therapist's approach to practice because of the decisions made in research designs.

Understanding what is missing in the literature can also be extremely clarifying. This is why most researchers will undertake a thorough literature review before conducting their studies. Therefore, being aware of the existing context for your research allows you to develop a rationale for your own study by identifying what is already known and what is yet to be discovered. Since research usually aims to make an original contribution to knowledge, this is also necessary to ensure that you do not accidentally replicate an existing study. Although it can be beneficial to reproduce existing studies intentionally for purposes of scientific replication, it is not good practice to replicate studies by accident. Therefore, it is common (and advised, especially when conducting your first research project) to conduct a thorough literature review as an initial stage in a research project.[13]

Factor 3C: Preferred Data Types: Numbers and/or Words

Although there are many levels worthy of exploration within the matrix of choices that align with alternative inquiry paradigms (see Table 4.1, p. 36), the issue of words and numbers is one of the most illuminative factors to help you gain insight into your own epistemological stance. Do you believe that key stakeholders will be more influenced by words or numbers when listening to the results of research? Although it feels as though

---

[13] It should be noted that an *a priori* literature review is actually contraindicated in some paradigms. For example, when undertaking a participatory project and attempting to generate new theory, best practice involves learning about the most relevant and useful focus to gather from the participants themselves. Therefore, the researcher will attempt to bracket their pre-assumptions and worldviews about what research is needed and wait to hear the unique narratives from the people who have the lived experience. The researcher will then seek out related literature, as it is needed to clarify the direction and focus and to challenge or confirm emerging ideas from the data. This attempt to identify and bracket pre-assumptions can also be relevant when attempting to theorize from grounded data. Once again, the researcher waits until ideas emerge inductively before seeking existing theoretical explanations to challenge what is particular to the context and people they are researching. However, for the purposes of your first research project, a literature review will be indisputably helpful to arrive at an intriguing and realistic research question and associated method.

you are answering a question about what other people believe, the answer is often a reflection of what you have taken into your own belief systems. In Mateo's example, one could argue that there are two bodies of research in the field of adult oncology: one that is driven from a focus on medical aspects of the disease, and another that emphasizes the psychological impacts. It is easy then to assume that one would prioritize numerical data (medical aspects) and the other would value narrative data (psychological impacts), but that is not the case, as interpretivist research is frequently occurring in hospitals. There are also studies conducted by physicians seeking to understand patient experiences in order to inform and improve their practice. The dominant approach in medical contexts is undoubtedly objectivist, however, and numbers are the most logical expression of deductive logic.[14] Mateo's decision to focus on numbers or words is not predetermined—it is a choice that he is privileged to make as a graduate music therapy student. Fortunately, the choice and corresponding privilege are often also yours, regardless of the context (although we discuss context as an influential factor in the next chapter).

An emphasis on numbers is well matched to methods such as pre- and posttest designs, where a difference in scores suggests that change has resulted from the therapeutic intervention. It also aligns with comparative designs (such as randomized controlled trials) that compare the benefits of one type of intervention over another (or no treatment/treatment as usual) based on measures taken. Many of the forms of analysis that are used in these designs have requirements about how much change is needed in order for it to be considered the result of the intervention (i.e., statistical significance); otherwise, the change—or lack thereof—in numbers could just as easily be due to coincidence. The demands for a large number of participants (i.e., sample size) in objectivist research may even influence your choice about the kind of study you will conduct. Many scholars will agree that recruiting participants with certain characteristics to take part in a research study can be difficult. Thus, it may not be possible to recruit enough participants to provide a study with the adequate statistical power required for a major research article in a top-tier journal. However, we contend that this should not discourage you from objectivist research, as data may be used by other researchers to advance the knowledge with the profession, and perhaps may be eventually pooled with data from other studies in a meta-analysis.

An emphasis on words often negates the need for large numbers, since this form of research seeks to make meaning by elaborating new understandings of people's

---

[14] Deductive reasoning is based on a logic that has a top-down approach, beginning with the most general and then progressing to the specific. Inductive reasoning works in the other direction, prioritizing understanding about individual experiences and then building toward generalizations. Typically, deductive reasoning is related to positivism and is based on the epistemological belief in objective truth, or verifiable truths. Inductive reasoning emphasizes the value of beginning with local and contextual knowledge of individuals and then begins to build toward generalizations. In terms of research, deductive research is often used to test a theory, whereas inductive research is more often used to build a theory.

experiences and also produces a lot of data, at least by word-count.[15] Interviews have been used in music therapy research as a popular way of gathering people's perspectives on and experiences of a particular phenomenon. An interpretivist researcher will then work carefully through all the different descriptions generated in the interview to make meaning from the words. This usually occurs through an inductive process in which themes or categories that seem to emerge from the data are identified. This requires contemplating multiple possibilities for interpreting the interviewee's words and reflexively considering the ways in which the researcher's pre-assumptions are shaping the construction of those categories. A researcher who is more interested in objective truth might conduct the same number of interviews and be equally satisfied that there are enough words/pages of data. However, this researcher would more likely allocate the data into predetermined categories to investigate whether their expectations about the phenomenon are confirmed. This is a more deductive approach to data analysis. If the researcher is still interested in numbers after working with the narrative data, they can always add a layer of numerical analysis, such as calculating how many interviewees' opinions are represented in each category, and which categories were the most frequently identified. In the continuing vignette, Mateo also considers the option of collecting data through interviews.

---

[15] This does not mean that numbers are irrelevant when collecting interview data, only that there is no "right" number needed to satisfy the design requirements. The concept of *saturation* (a term that has been introduced through grounded theory researchers) is often a more useful way of determining when enough data have been gathered from interviews. Saturation might be achieved when the researcher feels they are no longer identifying new possibilities in the data or cannot recruit any more informants to provide descriptions about the experience. It provides a useful alternative to predicting the necessary number of people early in the design of a project.

After Mateo decided to collect the quantitative self-report of patients concerning the effect of his music therapy sessions on fatigue, he began to question this decision and wondered if it would make more sense to let people describe their experiences more freely through interviews. This doubt occurred after he attained the two validated tools he was interested in using to measure fatigue. Matteo became nervous about using them, as the questions seemed negative and detached and he was worried that patients in the study might even feel worse after completing them. Could circling numbers on a sheet of paper accurately depict fatigue? Would there be risks to the integrity of the research that are associated with having patients complete pre- and posttests? His advisors suggested that he role-play the different options of self-report quantitative questionnaires and interviews with some of his graduate student peers and observe how they responded. Mateo decided to test the two quantitative self-report measurement tools he had found and also try interviewing his peers in an attempt to help him make this decision.

The role plays using self-report instruments quantitatively measuring fatigue seemed to go well and his peers reported that they felt okay when answering those questions. However, asking his peers directly about fatigue during extended interviews seemed to have more negative effects that Mateo had not anticipated. During the interviews, his peers seemed to be surprised by the negative focus on their fatigue levels and appeared to grow more fatigued in talking about it and trying to explain the experience of it. Piloting the different options had given him some insight into what the study was going to be like, both for his patients and from his own perspective as the researcher and interviewer. After carefully considering the various options, Mateo ultimately decided to remain focused on fatigue using the validated measures, which had been acceptable to his peers, and to compare their scores before and after improvisational music therapy and songwriting. Mateo shifted his research focus to: *The purpose of this study is to determine if improvisational or songwriting music therapy interventions have greater impact on self-reported fatigue levels for patients with cancer.*

Some researchers in this situation might consider that mixed methods would provide a convenient solution to aspects of Mateo's dilemma. Incorporating a mixed methods design would allow him to generate two data strands (qualitative and quantitative) on the topic of fatigue and would provide him with material if there was a non-significant result from analysis of the quantitative data. However, mixed methods research is not designed to have one data strand as a type of "back up." Rather, the focus of mixed methods research is on pursuing a singular research focus that integrates qualitative and quantitative data in ways that allow greater insight into a phenomenon. If an objectivist approach is taken, then the data cannot be discarded or disregarded if they do not provide the desired (i.e., statistically significant) results. If an interpretivist approach is adopted, then the quantitative measures need to be carefully aligned to the focus of the interviews, not the other way around. When he was testing the tools with his peers, Mateo observed that they did not want to talk about how music therapy had addressed their fatigue and instead wanted to talk about the emotional and relational dimensions of sharing musical experiences. An interpretivist researcher would allow this to direct the focus of the study, rather than have it predetermined by expectations, as it should be in objectivist research.

Conclusion

Beliefs we have about knowledge often feel like inevitable truths. It is no simple endeavor to own your preferences for forms of knowledge as choices, rather than as statements of facts. As illustrated by the example of Mateo, many influences shape what we consider to be strong and influential research: What makes it convincing? What makes it compelling? What is going to be most popular with key stakeholders in the context in which we practice as music therapists? Thus, there is nothing so simple as the best way to conduct research. It is your choice to privilege the power of number over the power of words, or vice versa. What you choose to notice in the literature influences your decisions about the best types of data to collect. Ultimately, it is also your choice to decide what influences to prioritize—from the range of teachers, experts, and literature from which you learn. All these layers inform what you decide to emphasize in your first research project and beyond. However, whereas these choices are influenced by a number of factors, we believe you should always be guided by your belief system and worldview to create an intrinsically motivating research project.

In this chapter, we have illustrated some strategies for uncovering your preferences for types of knowledge and forms of data. We highlight many hidden factors that may influence your decisions. By identifying your response to the various layers, you will gain greater clarity about the type of data you want to collect, why you are collecting those data, and, ultimately, how you will analyze them. For the purposes of this book, we have focused on data types, since other books, such as *Music Therapy Research* (Wheeler & Murphy, 2016), canvass an array of designs. As you come to terms with an array of influences on your thinking prior to finally choosing your preferred type of data and associated design, we hope you will be more satisfied by the first research experience that you have and potentially be excited to explore more in the future.

Chapter 5
Integrating Contextual Influences
to Develop a Feasible Project

Chapter Objectives

Chapter Objectives

At the conclusion of this chapter, you will have:

1. Explored how factors such as culture, gender, class, and privilege shape your research interests

2. Contemplated the organizational culture of the facility where you are interested in conducting research

3. Considered the emerging governmental policies and social movements that influence both clinical practice and research

Introduction

In the previous chapters of this text, we have explored how your personal experiences with music and health (Chapter 2), your beliefs and values (Chapter 3), and your worldview (Chapter 4) form hidden factors that can influence and shape your research. Being aware of these factors can facilitate the development of an intriguing and feasible first research project. What is missing from our discussion so far, however, is one of the most consequential factors: the unique contextual influences that act upon your research interests. These contextual influences are the focus of this chapter.

While it may be relatively easy—in theory, at least—to design a research project with unlimited resources, this is almost never the case. Researchers are often forced to make difficult decisions based on numerous factors that are often outside of their control. However, being aware of the contextual influences at play upon your project *before* you finalize your project design is an advantage and can help you in further refining your research question to ensure it is feasible and realistic. Therefore, in this chapter, you will learn about how organizational culture, government policies, and social movements all work in tandem to concomitantly impact your research project. In the next chapter, you will integrate these factors to inform how you write your research question.

In considering the societal and organizational influences around you, it is critical to understand that each of us experiences our contexts differently. Intersectional theory[1] provides one way of understanding how the opportunities you perceive are shaped by the dominant beliefs in your culture and community. As you consider the influence of organizational culture, government policies, and social movements, you might also reflect upon how someone who is different from you might experience the same factors. It may be that skin color shapes the way that government policies are implemented in different places. It may be that unconscious gender biases operate more blatantly in some types of organizational cultures. The ideas we present in this chapter are examples of large-scale influences that shape the kinds of research that will be accepted by your organization. There may be others, and we encourage you to consider those that stand out to you.

Because of the intersection between our own identity and the contextual parameters that influence our research questions and methods, we will use a single research topic to illuminate the different paths that researchers might take under varying conditions. We will draw on our own identities to illustrate the different positions we might adopt and encourage you to identify your own positions. We come from different countries, where diverse policy influences are at play. We also prefer different paradigmatic inquiry approaches, but we respect, support, and have genuine interest in one another's approaches. This may be because, despite our differences, we both are privileged in similar ways, being white-skinned, cisgender,[2] and tenured faculty members of research-intensive universities. From this rich palette of experiences, we have learned to appreciate the quality of a range of research approaches and have actively explored a number of them throughout our own research careers.

To illustrate how contextual influences inform the development of a research question and associated method, we have chosen the topic area of working with children with autism spectrum disorder (ASD) in a school setting. Despite our differences in approaches to research and practice, we share a sense of intrigue about the nature of the interaction between student[3] and music therapist, and our shared belief is that something about that

---

[1] Intersectional theory has reached prominence in many academic fields around the world. Based on the work of Kimberlé Crenshaw, intersectionality recognizes that we are not defined by only one aspect of our identity, but rather the intersection of a range of identifying features such as class, gender, ethnicity, sexuality, intellectual ability, etc. It is the unique combination of each of these aspects of identity that influences how discrimination is experienced.

[2] *Cisgender* is an adjective denoting or relating to a person whose self-identity conforms with the gender that corresponds to their birth/biological sex.

[3] We use the term *student* here as the young people are situated in a school context.

interaction is a key mechanism for therapeutic growth and change.[4] We have seen students spontaneously communicate and engage in social interactions within music therapy sessions wherein they share their voices, literally and metaphorically. For the purposes of this chapter, we draw on our curiosity about this phenomenon as the inspiration for exploring the influence of organizational cultures, policies, and social movements.

Layer 4: Contextual Influences

Factor 4A: Organizational Culture

One of the most crucial—yet frequently overlooked—aspects influencing the creation of your research question is the culture of the organization where the research is conducted. For many beginning researchers studying music therapy, the organization you approach will not be your employer, but an organization providing services related to the topic you have chosen. Therefore, it is useful to consider what the values of the organization are, as enacted in their organizational culture. Some organizations emphasize hierarchy and expert decision making, whereas others adopt a flexible management structure and emphasize collaboration. By examining these aspects of culture, you can also acquire a sense of what kinds of research might be favored and consider whether those align with your own research design preferences. You might then choose to shape your research question and associated method so that it somehow enhances the mission of the facility. Or you might recognize that the research focus you adopt will be different to the preferences of the organization and therefore will require more explanation and discussion in order to be approved. The interaction between the organization and a researcher's question is a delicate dance, as the researcher's question and the interests of the facility are both important and need to be considered among the many decisions made concerning your research project.

In the following example, we take into consideration the fact that education services for students with autism spectrum disorder (ASD) differ enormously around the globe. This is true among countries, but also within countries as large as the United States, where different states have distinct priorities. The context in which a music therapist works with a student may vary from mainstream schooling settings to specialized schools and to services that are independent of the education sector. The organizational culture of a special education setting is often quite different from the values of a mainstream school. Although student learning will always be the priority, the typical identity of a student in a special school differs on a number of levels from a typical student in mainstream education.

---

[4] It is no coincidence that both of us work closely with colleagues who are specialists in the field of music therapy and autism spectrum disorder: Dr. Grace Thompson at the University of Melbourne in Australia, and Professor Edward T. Schwartzberg at the University of Minnesota. We acknowledge their influence upon and shaping of our beliefs and ideas here.

The decision about whether to investigate a topic in a special school or a mainstream school therefore significantly changes the context surrounding the research.

Mike says:	Kat says:
In the United States, inclusion is a priority and therefore most students with ASD will attend mainstream schools and receive some degree of specialist service, depending on their Individualized Educational Programs (IEPs).	In Australia, special schools continue to exist as an alternative to the mainstream education system. Families are able to choose where they send their child for schooling, or they may combine access with two or three days in each context.
I agree that being a part of everyday school life is important for all children. Children with special needs should be visible in these contexts and integrated into the daily routine of schools. It is therefore a priority that students are able to develop social skills that will allow them to interact with other children in the classroom as well as on the playground. Music can provide particularly powerful conditions for developing and practicing social skills, because students are motivated and engaged and there is less reliance on traditional verbal interactions. Opportunities for success in music-based environments are abundant.	I enjoy working in special schools because the focus is less fixated on academic outcomes, and well-being has often been a priority in the special schools where I have worked. Although I recognize that social skills and communication are critical aspects of children's lives, I am also aware that teachers and speech-language therapists are usually focused on these skills. It is less common for members of the team to target quality of relationships, and therefore I often choose this focus to complement and extend the work of the interdisciplinary team.
Due to many complex factors in the United States, there is a greater likelihood of funding for music therapy services in these contexts if there is evidence that it will result in observable and measurable outcomes. It would seem that music therapy would provide ideal conditions for increases in the number and frequency of social interactions by children with ASD, as compared to other non-music therapy conditions. The IEP managers sometimes question whether there are data to support this conjecture, however. I would like to address this through research.	Families are often involved in setting goals for their child within special schools, and in my experience, they are often worried that their child will not be able to make friends or form relationships with caregivers in the future. They want their child to feel understood and heard, so they do not become emotionally isolated, especially if they are to become independent and live beyond the family unit in the future. This makes me want to focus on relationships through research.

The previous scenario highlights the difference between organizational cultures in special schools as compared to receiving specialist services in mainstream schools. What is also clear in our descriptions is that these contextual factors interface with our own beliefs and values (see Chapter 3), as well as our worldviews (see Chapter 4). Together, these inform our perceptions of what is important within the organizational culture.

It is also clear from these descriptions that music therapists often practice in the context of teams within organizations, and this powerfully shapes the decisions we make about where to focus our practice and research. Whether we decide it is important to compare the relative merit of our work with others, or to address the gaps in service provision—these are two different responses to the realization that music therapy with students with ASD rarely happens in isolation. These are not the only two options, as we could have investigated collaborative work with interdisciplinary team members, or consulted with managers about what kind of research would be most valuable for them. There are myriad possibilities in every context. What is important for your research, however, is recognizing the powerful influence of organizational culture. In doing so, you are able to make more informed and specific decisions about your research focus.

The funding of services within organizations also inevitably influences our decisions about research. In a competitive funding environment, where we may feel a need to prove that our services are as good as, or better than, those of our non-music therapy colleagues, contributing some sort of evidence[5] may feel like an obligation. By contrast, a context where interdisciplinary or even transdisciplinary practice is emphasized might lead us to feel that comparative designs could be perceived as competitive or unnecessary by our colleagues. As a researcher, you always have the freedom to choose your focus, and there is never only a single correct choice about design in response to contextual factors. It is just as possible to subvert power structures with the generation of new knowledge as it is to respect them. By revealing new knowledge about a phenomenon, you can either challenge the assumptions that evidence is based on or confirm that those assumptions are relevant and important. If the results are powerful enough, you can demonstrate that an intervention is effective and refute any claims that there is no need for music therapy services. But, as with each of the previous chapters, it is important to be conscious of the decisions you are making to ensure that you are committed to the project on which you will spend your time.

Factor 4B: Government Policies

Some policy influences occur at an international level, with bodies such as the United Nations making recommendations about the rights of diverse persons to equitably access services. A number of music therapists have described how they have been informed by

---

[5] We believe "evidence" can take many forms including, but not limited to, qualitative, quantitative, arts-based, anecdotal, and testimonial.

these international policies and integrated them into their research designs when arguing against constraints that exist within their own countries.[6] However, most international influences need to be embedded in national policies before they have the power to be called upon in making decisions about research directions.

The way that the government officials in each nation interpret, or choose to ignore, international policy directives varies greatly around the globe. This is partly because compliance or defiance may be more congruent with the dominant cultural ideology in each country but also depends on the particular political party in government at any given time. In addition, policies are constantly in flux, and there is often a long delay before a change in government policy trickles down into organizations and is actively implemented. Although this delay occurs in practice, as a researcher, you need to be more conscious of emerging policy influences, since your findings are aimed at the future. Research can take time to design, to be approved, to conduct, and a surprisingly long time to publish, so a lack of awareness could mean you produce findings that are irrelevant by the time they are disseminated.

One government policy that has impacted a wide range of music therapy practices is the directive toward evidence-based practice. Although initially established in the medical sector as a way to ensure that practitioners remained abreast of the latest discoveries relevant to their field, it has become a much more powerful influence over service funding and provision than could have been anticipated, particularly in the United States. This desire for evidence has also influenced the education sector, community-based programs, and prevention as well as intervention.[7]

In essence, an evidence-based framework privileges one form of knowing over others and has come to be primarily associated with objectivist approaches that utilize quantitative data, randomization, and control conditions. Although a range of types of evidence is

---

[6] For example, Daphne Rickson and Penny Warren (2017) draw on the United Nations Conventions on the Rights of Persons with Disabilities, and Lucy Bolger and Kat McFerran (2013) emphasize doctrines of Sustainability from the World Health Organization. Hans Petter Solli, Randi Rolvsjord, and Marit Borg (2013) highlight the international recovery movement in arguing against an exclusive focus on traditional quantitative evidence in the context of the mental health sector.

[7] Since it has become a longstanding influence within most capitalist and socialist systems, several music therapy theorists have provided commentary on the relative merits and limitations of evidence-based policymaking (Abrams, 2010; Aigen, 2015; Edwards, 2005). Each of these authors has provided a compelling argument against prioritizing certain research paradigms.

contained within various hierarchies,[8] all forms of subjective knowledge are located at the bottom, whether such knowledge involves qualitative data informed by user perspectives and experiences or expert opinion. Since all types of scientific evidence are relevant to making informed clinical decisions within evidence-based practice, Powers (2005) argued that it is necessary for clinicians to acquire the ability to appreciate interpretivist and objectivist research as viable evidence, while Rubin (2008) claimed that "different research hierarchies are needed for different types of EBP questions" (p. 56). Similarly, Pearson (2002) noted, "Best practice should reflect the whole range of evidence available—both quantitative and qualitative" (p. 21). However, in countries where funding is based on evidence, and evidence is established through studies with randomized control conditions, this policy has had real-world implications for professions such as music therapy that combine art and science. In the following example, we each approach this differently, partly influenced by the national policies in our countries, but also by our beliefs, values, and worldviews.

---

[8] Silverman (2010) compared various levels of evidence and noted that whereas numerous evidence hierarchies exist, these hierarchies rank studies in a similar manner based on the study design. These rankings are often depicted in a triangle indicating systematic reviews and meta-analyses of randomized controlled trials at the highest level of evidence. Studies including subjective data, along with expert opinion and service user experiences, are ranked near the bottom and indicate lower levels of evidence. Also see the Oxford Centre for Evidence-Based Medicine (2017).

Mike says:	Kat says:
In the United States, decision making about service provision for students with ASD is frequently based on *quantitative* evidence. Therefore, it is important that I design a study that will provide the type of evidence that funders require, since my goal is to increase access to clinical services for people with ASD.	Funding in the Australian system is still largely determined by school leaders who have to distribute their budget over a range of services, in which music therapy is often considered an added extra. Although decision makers often ask for "evidence," they use the term loosely and are usually interested in hearing about what research has shown, rather than whether the right kind of methodology was used to satisfy the evidence-based criteria.
A study that investigates social skills needs to provide quantitative evidence that music therapy is more effective than the current interventions students with ASD are receiving or treatment as usual. It would be feasible to compare student responses in the music therapy treatment to a non-music condition. Therefore, I could use a single-subject complete reversal (ABAB) design to show that it works repeatedly and is not a one-time or singular effect.	A study that investigates the nature of the relationships formed between the student and the music therapist could provide insight into why relationships are important, both now and in the future. It would help music therapists be able to articulate the benefits of a humanistic approach to music therapy, in which the therapist follows the interest of the student and encourages and matches their spontaneous musical expression. This is important, since being engaged and happy is not always a sufficient justification for funding music therapy.
By demonstrating superior and repeated benefit, I am attempting to provide the members of the interdisciplinary treatment team responsible for the IEP with quantitative data to continue music therapy services for a child with ASD in this educational setting.	By analyzing the nature of the relationship and the ways in which music creates conditions that foster meaningful relationships, I should be able to provide a more cogent explanation about the potential long-term benefits of quality relationship formation in the future.

These two responses to the evidence-based framework highlight how differently it can be interpreted, and how international policies are shaped within cultures—both at the level of a nation, down to the decisions made within a school. If you are trying to design a project that will influence the principal's decisions about service provision, it is critical to understand how that particular principal is interpreting what "evidence" means, since it is not always the same thing. As researchers and practitioners, the examples above illustrate how we hold different views on this. Although he may not agree with nor like it, Mike works in a country and in settings where knowledge produced by objective and measurable factors is required, which is in keeping with the scientific rules of evidence-based practice, objectivism, as well as the requirements of the school and its administrators. Kat suggests that scientific understandings of evidence are different from what is understood to be evidence in schools, where busy school leaders are making managerial decisions based on a range of factors, including the needs of their team as well as the best evidence available to determine services. Although this difference in opinion might reflect cultural differences shaping the decision makers, it also reflects our own understanding of the cultural norms in our country, which might actually be variable across different states and individual schools. This should illustrate to you that there is no single research design that is "right" in any context. Instead, it highlights the importance of knowing how your own experiences, and those of key decision makers in your context, can shape the decisions you make. Once again, being aware of these allows you to make informed decisions, rather than just guessing.

Factor 4C: Recognizing Emerging Social Movements

Social movements mark changes in cultural beliefs that have been previously accepted as facts. Just as paradigm shifts in research are responses to changing beliefs about what knowledge is most important, social movements reflect changing beliefs about people, power, and rights. The emergence of new social movements is often marked by changing language, as demonstrated by the change from referring to "retarded people" to "people with intellectual and developmental disabilities"—a phrase that purposefully puts the person first, before any identity marker of disability. More recently, person-first language has been challenged by people who are proud to identify with their unique features and prefer to be identified by their disability (i.e., autistic people). Music therapists often work with, and conduct research with, people whose rights are compromised by social structures that privilege a thin depiction of human existence considered to be "normal." This may include the negative associations of having a mental illness, or the financial challenges for governments that result from increasing numbers of people having heart disease or dementia. In many cases, the result of being categorized as "the other" instead of the norm is that people are not treated equitably. If you consider these factors when designing your research project, you will be able to make conscious decisions about how to refer to the people in your research. You can choose whether to align with the emerging social movements that are happening in your field, or to remain with traditional practices.

Neurodiversity provides a contemporary example of an emerging social movement in the field of disability studies that is relevant to the research topic we are illustrating in this chapter. Some people with lived experience of ASD argue that "being wired" differently has been socially constructed as a problem when, in fact, it is not a problem but another expression of human diversity.[9] As researchers in this field, we need to identify where we position ourselves in relation to emerging waves of thinking such as neurodiversity, as seen in the following example. Holding a conservative position based on what has been politically acceptable until now might be safer in the short term, but could be damaging in the long term. Alternately, attaching to every new social movement could prove problematic when some achieve significance but others have minimal impact. In the following examples, we each consider how acknowledging neurodiversity would influence the shape of our research projects.

---

[9] A special edition of the open-access music therapy journal *Voices: A World Forum for Music Therapy* (2014) focuses on disability, with neurodiversity being a particularly prominent theme in the discourse. Several authors explain how traditional approaches to autistic people have been extremely problematic for those receiving services and particularly in relation to the validity of their artistic expression.

Mike says:	Kat says:
The complete reversal design (ABAB) research project I have designed is based on a number of assumptions about what are considered to be appropriate social skills for young people. By expanding my research team to include a number of autistic people[10] as consultants, I can clarify whether the measures I have chosen to capture social skill development are considered relevant. Although the participants in my study are verbal, the concept of neurodiversity suggests that other people with ASD are better able to determine what is important socially than I am, since my assumptions are based on neurotypical experiences.	Young people with lived experience of disability are well placed to determine the kinds of programs that are meaningful to them. This is particularly true when it comes to understanding why the relationships that are established in music therapy are valuable to them. Since the young people I have planned to engage in my study are nonverbal, I will need to interpret what is meaningful to them by carefully reflecting on their behavioral responses. I will also incorporate the intuited understandings of the music therapist and parents who have experience of being in relationship with them.
Before commencing the study, I will consult with and pay a committee to examine the behaviors I plan to measure and to examine some pilot footage of music therapy sessions. Based on their feedback, I will identify which behaviors I will measure across the study and the kinds of changes for which I may be looking.	To do this, I will first identify moments in the session that the music therapist experienced as meaningful, on the assumption that connectedness in relationship is felt by both persons. I will then examine the young person's experience in that moment based on how they appear to respond.
This is likely to generate more meaningful data than those based on neurologically normative assumptions but still allows me to meet the required standards for quantitative evidence-based research that will lead to better understandings about music therapy service provision for autistic young people in schools.	Since the participants in this study are young and many are engaged in family life, I will also invite parents to report on their perceptions of those moments identified as meaningful and incorporate their ideas into my analysis.

These examples illustrate that acknowledging neurodiversity does not necessarily demand a particular type of research. New ways of thinking can be incorporated into traditional designs, or they can be aligned with a critical paradigm that intentionally

---

[10] These consultants requested to be referred to as "autistic people" and I am honoring their desire.

challenges traditions and assumptions. However, acknowledgment does influence whose knowing is considered to be more important and may shift the focus from the researcher to those who have lived experience of the condition being researched. In particular, being aware of emerging social movements means being more active in reflecting on how privileged we are, particularly in comparison to the persons with whom we work. It suggests that we seek out alternative perceptions in those areas most likely associated with our assumptions about what is important, and that we remunerate people for their participation, rather than expect it to be donated.

The final layer of influences that we have described focuses on the most external factors that nonetheless shape the focus of our research question and associated method. This does not suggest that the locus of influence is distant from your own personal beliefs and values, since we have highlighted how the external and internal intersect with one another. Each individual will experience organizational culture, social movements, and policies differently because of their status within the system. This flows in two directions, since it includes the degree to which you choose to be influenced by these external factors, as well as how you are perceived by those with power within the system. Issues such as gender, race, sexual identity, and cognitive capacity will all shape this encounter.

For us, the result is quite different, despite the many identity features we share. As the following purpose statements illustrate, the research studies we are proposing reflect our differences more than our similarities in values. Yours would also uniquely reflect the beliefs and values that you bring to the project, combined with your understanding of the external factors that shape your decisions.

Integrating Contextual Influences into Research Purposes and Questions

Now that we have both objectivist and interpretivist research threads, the next step is to write a purpose statement. Purpose statements tend to be broader than research questions, and it is therefore helpful to write purpose statements before attempting to write research questions. However, it is imperative to understand that writing purpose statements (and research questions) is an iterative process—your initial purpose statement will likely go through a number of revisions. Similarly, writing an elegant research question is extremely difficult and typically requires a number of iterations before it is finalized. Whereas it is acceptable to have more than one research question, having too many research questions can dilute the focus and purpose of your study. We recommend writing a single research question for your initial project, as this may help to augment the focus of the study.

Mike's Research Purpose Statement:	Kat's Research Purpose Statement:
The purpose of this study is to determine if music therapy is more effective at promoting the development of social skills than a non-music therapy social skills training intervention.	The purpose of this study is to explore the experiences of musical relationship between six autistic young people and their music therapists.
I will use video analysis (including reliability measures) to count the number of times the behaviors identified by the research team are displayed in each condition within a complete reversal design.	I will combine video and interview analysis informed by phenomenological methods to develop a rich description of what makes the experience meaningful.
Mike's Objectivist Research Question:	**Kat's Interpretivist Research Question:**
Are there differences in social skills as measured by the number of spontaneous verbalizations in non-music and active music creation conditions with 8- to 10-year-old students with autism spectrum disorder?	How do six autistic students and their music therapists appear to experience being in relationship together?

In the following chapter, we will draw together and synthesize all of the layers of influence that we have outlined in this and the preceding chapters. This will provide you with an opportunity to process what you have learned and to reflect on your own unique situation. Before that time, take a moment to consider these contextual influences and confirm where you would like to locate your research project. This will help to clarify how to write your research question and associated method.

Chapter 6
Synthesizing Personal Experiences, Beliefs and Values, Worldview, and Contextual Influence into a Refined Research Question

Chapter Objectives

At the conclusion of this chapter, you will have:

1. Reviewed the previous four major factors and 12 subfactors identified in Chapters 2–5 that influence research questions

2. Developed and written an epoché to tell your research narrative

3. Developed and written a purpose statement for your research project

4. Developed, written, and received feedback on an intrinsically intriguing and feasible research question

Introduction

It is our fundamental viewpoint that exploring the beliefs that shape what you will research leads to a more interesting and powerful research question. As a researcher with therapy training, you are well positioned to do this work, which is similar to examining unconscious issues, or exploring topics more deeply, in order to gain greater clarity and awareness. We have designed this book so that you are guided in a step-by-step fashion to explore those beliefs and values and, in doing so, to choose a research method that suits your beliefs and focuses on what is most important to you, as well as what is feasible for you in your current context.

This chapter is designed to remind you of what you have already processed as you read the book from beginning to end. However, if you are starting here, we suggest you may need to visit earlier chapters whenever the prompts are unclear to you, since we have provided a lot more detail earlier in the text. We have also provided illustrative examples of how we and others might explore our beliefs to help you understand what we mean, but those examples are not meant to be templates. Each one of you will design a unique research question that is based in your personal experiences, beliefs, and values, and combined with the current contexts in which your research will take place.

By the conclusion of this chapter, you should have generated your research question. Beneath that research question rest the many layers we have helped you identify. Not all of them will be immediately apparent, but they will reappear as you work through the details of your research design, and you can use those insights to inform the decisions that remain. To facilitate this process in the current chapter, we will briefly revisit aspects from each chapter as an opportunity to synthesize the many factors that influence your project. Please be aware that it is not a problem if some of your thoughts have changed from your initial reading of the chapters. In fact, it is helpful and insightful to change your thoughts throughout the process. In addition, although we think that all the factors are important and interesting, they may not all be necessary or appropriate for your particular research project. Therefore, please feel free to focus on the ones you are interested in and glean what you can from the process.

Chapter 2 focused on connecting to the intriguing personal experiences of music, health, and well-being that you have had and therefore feel inspired to investigate. Research inevitably involves hard work, and many of the tasks of research can be quite administrative, frustrating, and tedious. If you are captivated by your idea, you will more easily sustain yourself through these arduous moments. Although there is room for pragmatism in choosing your research focus, we believe it should come later (see Chapter 5), rather than earlier. If you begin with what inspires and intrigues you, you can slowly refine this to what will actually work.

So, to begin, we would like you to consider *and write*[1] your responses to the following questions:

1. Why did you enter the music therapy profession? What were the experiences that you had related to music, health, and well-being? What had you noticed about others' experiences of this?

2. Have you had intriguing experiences while observing or practicing music therapy? What occurred? Why is this of interest to you?

3. Have you been captivated by media representations of music, health, and well-being? How have you felt about these representations? How do you think the general public feels about these representations?

Chapter 3 focused on the beliefs and values you hold about music, health, and well-being. These beliefs often exist beneath your awareness, and you probably experience them as truths or facts about why music therapy is important. The purpose of Chapter 3

---

[1] Writing or typing responses to the proposed questions will help create a history of the project and how it evolves. Being able to come back to these responses is typically helpful when you start to question why you made certain decisions about the research.

was therefore to bring these beliefs and values into consciousness in order to examine them and consider whether they are part of what you will investigate. If you do not go through this process, your fundamental beliefs will still affect your choices about research design, but you will not be as clear about them. You will make assumptions about what will happen and may not be able to realize what actually occurs in your research project. We introduced the concepts of ontology, ethics, and aesthetics to help you explore and examine these beliefs and values.

The next step is to write your responses to the following questions, which may be even more insightful now that you have worked through the whole process described in the subsequent chapters.

> 1. What is it that makes therapy work? Is it more closely related to the therapeutic relationship, the music, or something else? How could that be reflected in what you consider to be important and interesting as a research topic?
>
> 2 Whose rights need to be considered in determining the focus of your research and during the therapeutic encounter? Are there some aspects of research design that would be too demanding or impinge on the benefits available to participants?
>
> 3. What do you find beautiful in music therapy, and how does that relate to your own musical decision making within the therapy process and the degree of consistency that might be necessary in your research project?

Chapter 4 focused on your worldview, or what you believe about the nature of knowledge and how knowledge should be acquired. We used the Great Debate between objectivism and interpretivism (previously referred to as *quantitative* and *qualitative*) to highlight the most common differences in worldview that have been represented in music therapy research textbooks. We asked you to explore how you developed your beliefs about what knowledge is most important by reflecting on whose opinions have been influential in your life. Although there are many layers that might have informed your epistemological stance, we focused on your university training, what you have read in the literature, and your own personal inclination toward numbers or words as the most convincing sources of knowledge.

Now it is time to consider these influences, combined with those beliefs you had already established prior to studying music therapy.

1. Which theoretical influences were most emphasized during your training to practice as a music therapist (humanism, behavioralism, medical models, psychodynamic approaches, critical thinking)? What were the preferred research methods during your music therapy academic training (interpretivist/objectivist, critical/empirical), and how have they shaped the types of data you value?

2. How has your reading of the existing literature impacted what type of data you are interested in collecting? Do the gaps in the literature intrigue you, or do you want to conduct research that is similar to what you have already read?

3. When you think about what kind of research is most important or powerful, do you think about needing the evidence provided by numbers or by the stories told with words? Is that what you focus on in music therapy practice as well, or is it different?

Chapter 5 focused on being aware of the context in which you plan to conduct your research. We suggested that different organizational cultures emphasize particular approaches to research. Medical settings are often influenced by basic biological research and therefore value other research that is conducted in similar ways. Community organizations often have an advocacy orientation that emphasizes consumer voice and collaborating with service users. And, of course, there is often mixed messaging about what is valued in practice and what is valued in research. The influence of higher-level policy might contribute to either the confusion or the clarity that organizations or emerging social movements have about what research is important. Being aware of how your own identity intersects with the values embodied by the organization where you will conduct your research is therefore important. It does not mean that you will always comply with the dominant view, but it does mean that you will know what to expect when you present your ideas to your supervisor, your advisor, and others who might think differently from you.

Understanding these contextual factors is helpful in making final decisions about why, how, and what you will investigate. To help gain clarity about this, we suggest using the following questions.

1. What does the organization where you will conduct your study value when it comes to research? What values are embedded in their practice orientation? What phrases or key words do they use to describe what is important to the organization?

2. What policies (including at the facility, local, and governmental levels) are influential in the context you want to research? Does the evidence-based paradigm dominate in your sector, or is its influence cursory?

3. What language is appropriate to use in describing the people who will participate in your research? Has that changed in response to emerging social movements, and, if so, have you been careful to embed those changes consistently in your writing and thinking?

The Three-Step Process to Writing Your Research Question

After reviewing the information presented in Chapters 2–5 and responding to the questions posed above, it is time to begin the process of crafting your research question. As this is one of the single most difficult tasks for beginning researchers, we believe taking the time to articulate an epoché can help to better refine your thoughts and determine *why* you are interested in doing what you are proposing. Including a *why statement*, such as an "I believe . . ." narrative, can make it personalized, relevant, and engaging.

Step 1: Creating an Epoché

Once you have thoughtfully considered each of the above questions, it is time to write some paragraphs that coalesce all of these influences into a story that describes why you are interested in conducting this research project. This will be a helpful reference as you prepare to make additional decisions. Moreover, it can serve as a reminder about *what* is important and *why* it is important to you. This is sometimes called an epoché and is a useful way of amalgamating everything you have learned about how hidden factors influence your particular research project. It might be a story that sounds something like this, with your specific answers added.

> When I first realized I needed to choose a research focus, I was not sure what to choose. When I reflected on *why* I entered the profession in the first place, I realized that . . . *<enter experience>*.
>
> What was most intriguing about that experience was . . . *<enter description>*.
>
> When I started to have experiences of music therapy, one of the things that really stayed with me was . . . *<enter description>*.
>
> The reason it stayed in my mind was . . . *<describe rationale>*.
>
> When I think about why these things have stayed with me, I realized that I believed . . . *<enter description>*.

Step 2: Creating a Purpose Statement

Having written your story about all of these hidden factors that might influence the general kinds of research questions you want to ask, you are ready to generate your purpose statement.[2] We suggest that you should first develop a purpose statement in the form of a declarative sentence summarizing the topic and goals of your research project. A purpose statement is often located at the conclusion of a literature review and may precede the research question and the method section.

> The purpose of this research is to . . . *<enter purpose statement here>*.

Step 3: Crafting a Research Question

The research question differs from the purpose statement in some fundamental ways. Most obviously, the research question is *asked* rather than stated. Therefore, the research question must be in question format, which is often a difficult task for beginning researchers. Additionally, the research question is more specific and may include contextual information about the study, as well as specific types of language that are suitable to represent those involved. Unlike the purpose statement, the research question often embeds key words that are related to the research design. For example, the use of the word *experience* often signifies a phenomenological project using an interpretivist approach; in contrast, highlighting a dependent measure such as *quality of life* might indicate an objectivist approach.

Every research question is different and unique. Just as we uniquely tailor music therapy programs to the specific needs of the individuals we meet, every research question is particular to the topic you want to investigate and how you want to investigate it. That is why two people can investigate the same people in the same context and still be radically different in approach, depending on what the researcher decides is important, ethical, and powerful. These intriguing factors have helped lead us to write a book to help you prepare to write a research question that is idiosyncratic to you, your interests, and your experiences. We believe there are a plethora of factors to consider in order for your research question to represent your personal beliefs, interests, and priorities, and being aware of these factors will ultimately lead to a stronger project.

Even having considered all of these factors, you should be aware that your research question will likely be edited many times as you refine your choices about the methods you will use to examine the question. The exact words—and their sequence—are important,

---

[2] We are purposely not including an example of a purpose statement or research question in an attempt to avoid providing models. The research question should be representative of your unique and idiosyncratic inquiry. However, there is no shortage of examples of research questions in the literature, as they are found in most articles. We recommend noticing how experienced researchers phrase their questions and their word choices, especially if you relate to their thinking, beliefs, and values.

and it is rare to be satisfied with your first attempts. As we previously noted, it is perfectly acceptable to have more than one research question or subsidiary questions, as long as they are related. However, having too many research questions can dilute the focus and purpose of your study. Having a singular research question is fine, especially for your first research project.

To help you generate your research question, we suggest considering the following points:

1. Be sure your research question is stated in question format.

2. Be certain your research question contains adequate context to orient the reader. For example, provide the reader with hints concerning what type of data will be collected and what is being studied.

3. Be sure your epoché, purpose statement, and research question are congruent with each other. These should successively narrow from general (epoché) to specific (research question).

4. Send your epoché, purpose statement, and research question to peers for supportive and critical feedback. Consider their critiques and integrate their feedback into your epoché, purpose statement, and research question.

<Enter research question here>

Conclusion

We wish you the best on your research journey. We appreciate that your mind will continue to process many issues related to recruitment, data collection, data analysis, and writing the paper. This text is designed to help you begin your journey with real insight into your own research inclinations. This process can be applied over and over as you design more research projects in the future, if that is where your career takes you. But in the meantime, we sincerely hope that this text makes your initial research journey feel exciting and important, and that the knowledge you generate, no matter how small it feels, helps you learn something more about the practice of music therapy.

References

Abbott, E. A. (2016). Reviewing the literature. In B. L. Wheeler & K. Murphy (Eds.), *Music therapy research* (3rd ed., pp. 56–65). Dallas, TX: Barcelona.

Abrams, B. (2010). Evidence-based music therapy practice: An integral understanding. *Journal of Music Therapy, 47*, 351–379. https://doi.org/10.1093/jmt/47.4.351

Aigen, K. (1995). Principles of qualitative research. In B. L. Wheeler (Ed.), *Music therapy research: Quantitative and qualitative perspectives* (pp. 283–311). Gilsum, NH: Barcelona.

Aigen, K. (2010). In defense of beauty: A role for the aesthetic in music therapy theory. *Nordic Journal of Music Therapy, 16*, 112–128. https://doi.org/10.1080/08098130709478181

Aigen, K. (2015). A critique of evidence-based practice in music therapy. *Music Therapy Perspectives, 33*, 12–24. https://doi.org/10.1093/mtp/miv013

Baker, F. A., & Young, L. (2016). The relationship between research and practice. In B. L. Wheeler & K. Murphy (Eds.), *Music therapy research* (3rd ed., pp. 26–36). Dallas, TX: Barcelona.

Biesta, G. (2007). Why "what works" won't work: Evidence-based practice and the democratic deficit in educational research. *Educational Theory, 57*(1), 1–22.

Bolger, L. E., & McFerran, K. S. (2013). Demonstrating sustainability in the practices of music therapists: Reflections from Bangladesh. *Voices: A World Forum for Music Therapists, 13*(2). https://doi.org/10.15845/voices.v13i2.715

Bonde, L. O. (2016). Letter to the editor: The black hole—or *is music a black box? Nordic Journal of Music Therapy, 25*, 105–106. https://doi.org/10.1080/08098131.2015.1111406

Bradt, J. (2015). Guidelines for publishing mixed methods research in the *Nordic Journal of Music Therapy. Nordic Journal of Music Therapy, 24*, 291–295. https://doi.org/10.1080/08098131.2015.1067065

Bradt, J., Burns, D. S., & Creswell, J. W. (2013). Mixed methods research in music therapy research. *Journal of Music Therapy, 50*, 124–148. https://doi.org/10.1093/jmt/50.2.123

Bruscia, K. E. (1998). Standards of integrity for qualitative music therapy research. *Journal of Music Therapy, 35,* 176–200.

Bruscia, K. E. (2014). *Defining music therapy* (3rd ed.). Dallas, TX: Barcelona.

Bryman, A. (2007). The research question in social research: What is its role? *International Journal of Social Research Methodology, 10,* 5–20. https://doi.org/10.1080/13645570600655282

Crenshaw, K. (1991). Mapping the margins: Intersectionality, identity politics, and violence against women of color. *Stanford Law Review, 43*(6), 1241–1299.

Creswell, J. W., & Plano Clark, V. L. (2011). *Designing and conducting mixed methods research* (2nd ed.). Thousand Oaks, CA: Sage.

Darrow, A. A. (2016). Developing a topic. In B. L. Wheeler & K. Murphy (Eds.), *Music therapy research* (3rd ed., pp. 47–55). Dallas, TX: Barcelona.

Dileo, C. (2000). *Ethical thinking in music therapy.* Cherry Hill, NJ: Jeffery Books.

Duke, R. A. (2010). 2010 Senior Researcher Award acceptance address: What if research was interesting? *Journal of Research in Music Education, 58,* 208–218. https://doi.org/10.1177/0022429410378029

Edwards, J. (2005). Possibilities and problems for evidence-based practice in music therapy. *The Arts in Psychotherapy, 32,* 293–301. https://doi.org/10.1016/j.aip.2005.04.004

Finlay, L. (2002). "Outing" the researcher: The provenance, process, and practice of reflexivity. *Qualitative Health Research, 12*(4), 531–545. https://doi.org/10.1177/104973202129120052

Finlay, L. (2009). Debating phenomenological research methods. *Phenomenology & Practice, 3*(1), 6–25.

Giorgi, A. (1997). The theory, practice, and evaluation of the phenomenological method as a qualitative research procedure. *Journal of Phenomenological Psychology, 28*(2), 253–260.

Gold, C., Solli, H. P., Kruger, V., & Lie, S. A. (2009). Dose-response relationship in music therapy for people with serious mental disorders: Systematic review and meta-analysis. *Clinical Psychology Review, 29,* 193–207. https://doi.org/10.1016/j.cpr.2009.01.001

Guba, E. G., & Lincoln, Y. S. (2005). Paradigmatic controversies, contradictions, and emerging confluences. In N. K. Denzin & Y. S. Lincoln (Eds.), *The Sage handbook of qualitative research* (3rd ed., pp. 191-215). London, UK: Sage.

Guillemin, M., & Gillam, L. (2004). Ethics, reflexivity and "ethically important moments" in research. *Qualitative Inquiry, 10,* 261–280.

Hiller, J. (2016). Epistemological foundations of objectivist and interpretivist research. In B. L. Wheeler & K. Murphy (Eds.), *Music therapy research* (3rd ed., pp. 99–117). Dallas, TX: Barcelona.

Jackson, N. (2016). Phenomenological inquiry. In B. Wheeler & K. Murphy (Eds.), *Music therapy research* (pp. 441–422). Dallas, TX: Barcelona.

Kenny, C. (2006). *Music and life in the Field of Play: An anthology.* Gilsum, NH: Barcelona.

Koch, T. (1995). Interpretive approaches in nursing research: The influence of Husserl and Heidegger. *Journal of Advanced Nursing, 21*(5), 827–836.

Kuhn, T. (1962). *The structure of scientific revolutions.* Chicago, IL: University of Chicago Press.

Lee, C. (2003). *The architecture of aesthetic music therapy.* Gilsum, NH: Barcelona.

Lincoln, Y. S., Lynham, S. A., & Guba, E. G. (2017). Paradigmatic controversies, contradictions, and emerging confluences, revisited. In N. K. Denzin & Y. S. Lincoln (Eds.), *The Sage handbook of qualitative research* (5th ed., pp. 108-150). Thousand Oaks, CA: Sage.

Luker, K. (2008). *Salsa dancing into the social sciences: Research in an age of info-glut.* Cambridge, MA: Harvard University Press.

Lykke, N. (2010). *Feminist studies: A guide to intersectional theory, methodology and writing.* New York, NY: Routledge.

Madsen, C. K. (1974). No one knows research but me. *Journal of Music Therapy, 11,* 169–180.

Malloch, S., & Trevarthen, C. (2009). *Communicative musicality: Exploring the basis of human companionship.* Oxford, UK: Oxford University Press.

Martin, D., & Loomis, K. (2007). Your philosophy of education. In D. Martin & K. Loomis (Eds.), *Building teachers: A constructivist approach* (pp. 38–68). Belmont, CA: Thomson Wadsworth.

McFerran, K. S., & Hunt, A. (2016). Funding research. In B. L. Wheeler & K. Murphy (Eds.), *Music therapy research* (3rd ed., pp. 92–98). Dallas, TX: Barcelona.

Mullins, G., & Kiley, M. (2002). 'It's a PhD, not a Nobel Prize': How experienced examiners assess research theses. *Studies in Higher Education, 27*, 369–386. https://doi.org/10.1080/0307507022000011507

Munhall, P. L., & Boyd, C. O. (1993). *Nursing research: A qualitative perspective* (2nd ed.). New York, NY: National League for Nursing Press.

New Zealand Qualifying Authority. (2014). *Degrees and related qualifications: Guidelines for programme approval and accreditation to provide programmes.* Wellington, NZ: Author.

Oxford Centre for Evidence-Based Medicine. (2017). *Levels of evidence.* Retrieved from http://www.cebm.net/oxford-centre-evidence-based-medicine-levels-evidence-march-2009/

Pearson, A. (2002). Nursing takes the lead. Refining what counts as evidence in Australian health care. *Reflections on Nursing Leadership, 28*(4), 18–21.

Powers, B. A. (2005). Critically appraising qualitative evidence. In B. M. Melnyk & E. Fineout-Overholt (Eds.), *Evidence-based practice in nursing and healthcare: A guide to best practice* (pp. 127–162). Philadelphia, PA: Lippincott Williams & Wilkins.

Rickson, D., & Warren, P. (2017). Music for all: Including young people with intellectual disability in a university environment. *Journal of Intellectual Disabilities.* https://doi.org/10.1177/1744629517701860

Roberts, M. (2006). Transitions from clinical experience to clinical questions and then research. *Voices: A World Forum for Music Therapy, 6,* 3. https://doi.org/10.15845/voices.v6i3.280

Rolvsjord, R. (2010). *Resource oriented music therapy.* Gilsum, NH: Barcelona.

Rubin, A. (2008). *Practitioner's guide to using research for evidence-based practice.* Hoboken, NJ: John Wiley & Sons.

Ruud, E. (2005). Philosophy and theory of science. In B. L. Wheeler (Ed.), *Music therapy research* (2nd ed., pp. 33–44). Phoenixville, PA: Barcelona.

Sacks, O. (1973). *Awakenings.* New York, NY: Harper Perennial.

Schmidt, L. K. (2016). *Understanding hermeneutics.* London, UK: Routledge.

Silverman, M. J. (2009). The effect of single-session psychoeducational music therapy on verbalizations and perceptions in psychiatric patients. *Journal of Music Therapy, 46,* 105–131. https://doi.org/10.1093/jmt/46.2.105

Silverman, M. J. (2010). Applying levels of evidence to the psychiatric music therapy literature base. *The Arts in Psychotherapy, 37,* 1–7. https://doi.org/10.1016/j.aip.2009.11.005

Solli, H. P., Rolvsjord, R., & Borg, M. (2013). Toward understanding music therapy as a recovery-oriented practice within mental health care: A meta-synthesis of services users' experiences. *Journal of Music Therapy, 50,* 244–273. https://doi.org/10.1093/jmt/50.4.244

Stige, B., Malterud, K., & Midtgarden, T. (2009). Toward an agenda for evaluation of qualitative research. *Qualitative Health Research, 19*(10), 1504–1516. https://doi.org/10.1177/1049732309348501

Stige, B., & Strand, R. (2016). Philosophical inquiry. In B. L. Wheeler & K. Murphy (Eds.), *Music* therapy research (3rd ed., pp. 672–684). Dallas, TX: Barcelona.

Tsiris, G. (2008). Aesthetic experience and transformation in music therapy: A critical essay. *Voices: A World Forum for Music Therapy, 8*(3). https://doi.org/10.15845/voices.v8i3.416

Tsiris, G., Farrant, C., & Pavlicevic, M. (2014). *A guide to research ethics for arts therapists and arts and health practitioners.* Philadelphia, PA: Jessica Kingsley.

Viega, M., & Forinash, M. (2016). Arts-based research. In B. L. Wheeler & K. Murphy (Eds.), *Music therapy research* (3rd ed., pp. 491–504). Dallas, TX: Barcelona.

Voices: A World Forum for Music Therapy, 14(3). (2014). Special issue on music therapy and disability studies. https://www.voices.no/index.php/voices/issue/view/82

Wheeler, B. L. (Ed.). (2005). *Music therapy research* (2nd ed.). Gilsum, NH: Barcelona.

Wheeler, B. L., & Bruscia, K. (2016). Overview of music therapy research. In B. L. Wheeler & K. Murphy (Eds.), *Music therapy research* (3rd ed., pp. 1–9). Dallas, TX: Barcelona.

Wheeler, B. L., & Murphy, K. (Eds.). (2016). *Music therapy research* (3rd ed.). Dallas, TX: Barcelona.